PRACTICAL GUIDE SERIES

THE PRIMARY
P·E·R·F·O·R·M·A·N·C·E
HANDBOOK

Gaynor Davies

Ward Lock Educational Co. Ltd.

WARD LOCK EDUCATIONAL CO. LTD.
BIC LING KEE HOUSE
1 CHRISTOPHER ROAD
EAST GRINSTEAD
SUSSEX RH19 3BT

A MEMBER OF THE LING KEE GROUP
HONG KONG • SINGAPORE • LONDON • NEW YORK

© 1995 Ward Lock Educational Co. Ltd.

© Text Gaynor Davies
All rights reserved. No part of this publication may be reproduced, stored in a retrieval system, or transmitted, in any form or by any means, electronic, mechanical, photocopying, recording or otherwise, without the written permission of the publisher.

First published 1995

ISBN 0 7062 5219 5

To Steve and Jack: my trusty backstage crew

The publisher wishes to thank the following for permission to make use of reference material:
Walker Books Limited for *Dear Greenpeace* ©1991 Simon James
Pavilion Books Limited for both *Touch the Moon* from *Fantastic Stories* by Terry Jones and for *The Serpent King* by Madhur Jaffrey. We are also grateful to Pavilion Books for permission to use the illustration on page 61 by Michael Foreman.
Photographs on pages 45, 48 are from the Mary Evans Picture Library; page 39 from AJS Ltd.

and the following for their help:
Alistair Black and the Hampshire Drama Advisory team.
Margaret Bunyard and the Hampshire County Wardrobe.
Jeff Higley.
Mark Morley and AJS Theatre Lighting and Stage Supplies, Hampshire.
The Hampshire History Advisory team.
Staff and pupils of schools in Hampshire and London.

Artwork is by Mike Komarnyckyj and Mick Stubbs.

Printed in Hong Kong

CONTENTS

1. Drama, Performance and the Primary Curriculum — 4
2. Introduction — 6
3. The Instant School Assembly model *Cinderella* — 8

Projects

4. *The Nativity*
   a whole school project — 13

5. *Dear Greenpeace*
   a project for KS2 pupils — 29

6. *The Great Exhibition*
   a history-based drama project — 45

7. *The Serpent King*
   a mask project — 61

8. *The Shadow Puppet*
   a project for all ages particularly pupils with special needs — 80

9. Organising your performance — 93

10. Checklist — 99

Index — 103

DRAMA, PERFORMANCE AND THE PRIMARY CURRICULUM

Speaking and listening
"...Pupils should be encouraged to participate in drama activities, improvisation and performances of varying kinds, using language appropriate to a role or situation. They should be given opportunities to respond to drama they have watched, as well as that in which they have participated. (KSI)

"...Pupils should be given opportunities to participate in a wide range of drama activities, including improvisation, role-play and the writing and performance of scripted drama. In responding to drama, they should be encouraged to evaluate their own and others' contributions." (KS2)
From Programmes of Study for English, SCAA, 1995

In recent times Drama in the primary school has had a chequered career. The failure of curriculum planners to recognise it as a subject in its own right has led to its absorption and adoption by other subject areas: English, History, Technology, Science or Dance. There is, however, a gradual move back to the teaching of Drama as a separate subject area with its own curriculum structure and content. The Arts Council guidance on Drama in Schools 1992 (see page 5) has played a key role in returning Drama to mainstream curriculum planning. It provides a clear rationale for Drama, that of good classroom practice within a balanced pedagogy. This view is echoed in the 1995 National Curriculum Orders for Speaking and Listening within English.

The balance of practical activity and intellectual discipline promoted by the Arts Council document and supported by recent legislation from SCAA on English teaching is reflected in the rationale behind *The Primary Performance Handbook*. The Drama curriculum should blend development and exploration of the drama process through a range of practical activities, such as improvisation. The pupils acquire and develop a range of skills – for example, the use of mime, movement and gesture, within a small group or in front of an audience as a piece of performance work. The two aspects, theory and presentation, can stand alone, but together they provide a balanced dramatic curriculum that is accessible to all abilities and age ranges.

The Primary Performance Handbook sets out five major performance projects for primary school pupils. Each project is set within a curriculum framework, has a specific technical focus, and is based upon use of a range of drama processes in partnership between pupil and teacher. There are no scripts. These may evolve later as the drama develops. There are stories which form the basis of each project. Story is an excellent stimulus. Pupils love story, and there is a rich heritage to choose from. Strategies are given for developing these stories using simple drama approaches.

There is an end product – a performance. This can take a variety of forms:
- presenting the project to other classes in an informal setting.
- presenting the project in a whole school assembly.
- presenting the project as a whole school event to an audience of parents, friends and people from the local community.
- taking the project to a venue away from school: another school, a community centre, a hospital or local Arts centre.

Performance does not mean just a grand-scale event involving hundreds of people. It can be just as effective on a small scale to a selected group. You must be the judge of the most effective forum for the pupils.

Putting on a play and standing up in front of an audience can be a daunting experience for some pupils. It is important to bear this in mind when taking on one of these projects. Build up in small steps so that the confidence and skills of the performers grow with the project. The important element of this handbook is the value of developing the performance from a story base. The work has to come from the pupils. The teacher is the facilitator to begin with and takes over as director once the performance has taken shape. At this point you are developing and honing performance skills within a framework that belongs to the pupils. They have ownership of the material, language and movement. The vital point to grasp is the partnership between the project and the whole curriculum and between teacher/pupil and pupil/pupil.

Don't forget that some pupils thrive on the challenge of performing in public. Hidden talent can be revealed: not just as performers but also of technicians, designers, musicians or organisers. Parents enjoy watching their offspring perform whatever the venue. Some have been involved with their children performing from when they were very young. Others may not have had these opportunities before and thrive on the new challenge. Denying the opportunity to perform is to offer only half a drama curriculum. In providing a variety of platforms you enable pupils to have access to a range of exciting, challenging, and enjoyable learning experiences.

A school performance can add to the spiritual and cultural health of the school. It can bring together a variety of individuals who, by focusing on one event, learn a great deal about each other and the institution they work in. It can also be a celebration of achievement of the pupils' and teachers' work and of the teamwork involved in putting on the event and in developing a showcase to the world outside to share in the life and work of your school.

An exciting performance lasts a long time in the memory of those involved and in the life of the school.

'DRAMA IS AN ART, A PRACTICAL ACTIVITY AND AN INTELLECTUAL DISCIPLINE. IT INVOLVES THE CREATION OF IMAGINED CHARACTERS AND SITUATIONS WHICH ARE ENACTED WITHIN A DESIGNATED SPACE. A DRAMA EDUCATION WHICH BEGINS WITH PLAY MAY EVENTUALLY INCLUDE ALL THE ELEMENTS OF THEATRE. LIKE ALL THE ARTS, DRAMA HELPS US MAKE SENSE OF THE WORLD'.

Arts in Schools guidance on Drama education 1992

INTRODUCTION

How to use this book

Chapters 4 to 8 each contain a performance project with a specific technical focus. The projects can be carried out in any order. Each project can stand on its own, be followed through or be the basis for extracting ideas.

The projects give you guidelines for development, including storyline, scene structure, character outlines, and technical hints on staging the event. A short resources list is at the end of each project.

Each project is placed within a curriculum structure. It can stimulate or support a topic which could be broad based or subject-focused. Ideas for work are offered under subject headings in *Cross-Curricular Links*. They are ideas. It is up to you to develop as and when appropriate.

Each project is placed within a dramatic framework, as suggested by the Arts Council Guidance. In the section *Dramatic Curriculum* activities are related to:
- MAKING: Expressing ideas through a variety of dramatic forms and conventions: movement – the use of a still image which comes to life in a particular way.
- PERFORMING: Engaging and communicating with an audience in a range of performance modes: as a performer.
- RESPONDING: Appreciating, appraising and evaluating drama work: as a member of an audience watching a performance piece in assembly.

Each project has a story framework *Creating the Story* with ideas for creating and developing the story. A scene structure is set and ways of extending the scenes are also given.

The projects are based upon the technique of **improvisation**. This is a basic drama teaching technique. Pupils are set a task, usually within a time limit, and, in a group, act out a 'pretend' situation without a script. In improvisation, pupils take on roles and pretend to step into someone else's shoes. They act out ideas using their own words and their own movements which they feel are appropriate to the role. The pupils draw on their own knowledge and experience, projecting their own ideas to develop the role and ultimately the piece of drama.

The performance project is rooted in improvisation. The initial improvisations by the pupils then need to be crafted, redrafted, rehearsed and discussed and recorded until it becomes a prepared piece of work. The crafting process is a partnership between teacher and pupil.

A brief description of the projects

1) THE NATIVITY – a whole school performance project based on the stories of the animals who are at the manger to witness the birth of baby Jesus. Each animal has a tale to tell about their journey to Bethlehem. Ideas for staging are covered, as well as tips on organising a whole school performance. It is suitable for all ages and can be tackled by inexperienced pupils and staff.

This project would fit into a topic on Festivals or Celebrations and ideas for class based work activities are offered. Although this is based on a story from the Christian tradition, the structure can be adapted for other world religions which have a wealth of exciting stories to share to a wider audience. This project gives you the platform for developing such an event.

2) DEAR GREENPEACE – This is a project for top juniors who have had some experience in devising plays for performance in front of an audience. The piece is based on the children's book *Dear Greenpeace* by Simon James. It is a series of letters between a girl and the Greenpeace organisation. The project shows how you can develop a play from only two characters and from a series of letters. It offers ideas for a scene structure and adding characters to enhance the story and to extend it out into a play for a class size group.

It could be used to support an environmental or science based topic as it raises a number of issues which relate to these areas. Ideas for developing class work are given. This topic focuses on simple stage lighting techniques as well as a few staging tips.

3) THE GREAT EXHIBITION – This project gives you ideas for working on 'The Victorians' – a history unit for Key Stage 2 pupils. It is based on the events which surround the exhibition of 1851 at the Crystal Palace. The story is about the lives of people who visit the exhibition. They come from all parts of Victorian society and help to make a vast topic come to life. Curriculum links are offered and ideas for quick and simple costumes are described. The whole event culminates in a performance using one main dramatic idea: that of physical theatre where the actors not only create characters but the props and scenery just by using their bodies. In this case the pupils create the Crystal Palace in a simple but effective way. This project could lead to, and stimulate, work in this subject-based topic and provides a route through a large and exciting piece of work.

4) THE SERPENT KING – is a mask project based on an Indian folktale. This is for all ages and provides a different approach to developing and performing a story. Ideas for making simple masks are described. These could form part of your Technology or Art curriculum. The story is written in full and ideas for developing characters and extra scenes are also given. This project also gives some staging ideas and builds upon some of the ideas from previous projects. It is an exciting, colourful and highly effective way of turning a traditional folktale into a performance piece for an audience.

5) THE SHADOW PUPPET – This project gives plenty of ideas for developing the ancient art of shadow puppetry. Making a puppet and ways of using it to tell a story are described. Ideas for staging, the construction of a screen, lighting effects, special tricks and stories are given. In this project, nursery rhymes are used and one is described in detail. This project is geared to younger and less able pupils but can be adapted for all ages and skill levels. It's great fun, very simple and highly effective. It makes a useful addition to your Science, Art and Technology curriculum.

The projects are independent of one another and can be chosen in any order.

THE REST OF THIS BOOK

The chapter **Organising your performance** offers ideas, information and handy hints to help you organise your performance. The emphasis is on organisation, preparation, planning, communication, and delegation. Hints on timetabling, budgeting and roles are offered. Checklists and handy hints for an event without tears are described. All the information in this section is based on experience!

The basis of all the projects appears in the first chapter **THE INSTANT ASSEMBLY MODEL.** This is a piece of work that developed from the need of teachers to find different approaches to assemblies and from my own work in developing simple approaches for bringing stories to life. The techniques offered range from the basic use of the still image to more complex activating strategies for bringing the images to life. You can apply these to each project and make them as simple or as complex as you wish. The basic premise is to take a story, break it up into bite-size chunks and then use a range of strategies to put the story into performance mode, enhancing it with a range of technical effects.

All the projects are based on work that has been tried and tested in schools in London and Hampshire where I work as a member of the Drama Inspection and Advisory Services for Hampshire Education. So this is not 'pie in the sky' materials but work which has been tried and tested with a range of pupils and hardworking staff.

THE INSTANT SCHOOL ASSEMBLY MODEL

FIRST THOUGHTS

The word 'instant' in the title of this opening project should encourage you to try it out! It *is* instant and it can solve the pressure of coming up with new ideas for the weekly assembly. This project provides one answer to a recurring school problem, and it also provides the basis for this performance handbook.

The method at its simplest level is: find a story, break it up into suitable scenes, give each group/class a scene, rehearse, and perform. The method can also provide a range of learning opportunities which will enhance drama work in your school as well as give a platform for further research into other curricular areas.

You can do it as a performance – a one-off event or you can use it to stimulate a term of project-based enquiry work on a particular theme, topic or cross curricular dimension. You can make it as hard or as easy as you wish. It all depends on your intention. Take the model, try it out and see how it works. Only by 'getting inside' the structure, will you see how it works and how you can extend it to challenge the pupils and enhance their learning.

The model can be done just through simple still or frozen pictures or you can use some basic activating or "bringing to life" strategies to deepen the content and challenge the pupils.

Try it, step by step and all will be revealed.

INTRODUCTION

A typical school scenario:
It is time, yet again, for your class assembly. You are snowed under with assessments or reports. You have to prepare for a visit by inspectors. There are parent consultations to arrange. Next weekend is the school fair, you are also moving classrooms and the sink is blocked. The last thing you or your pupils need is an assembly but then you remember your secret weapon:

THE INSTANT ASSEMBLY MODEL
- ✔ Quick.
- ✔ Effective.
- ✔ Involves the whole class.
- ✔ Needs very little preparation.
- ✔ Will make the other classes sit up, watch and learn.
- ✔ Will not make everyone (pupil or teacher!) dissolve into tears at the thought of yet another assembly.
- ✔ A life saver.

For the Instant Assembly Model you will need:

(i) The class split into sensible working groups of 5 or 6.
(ii) The pupils acquainted with some basic drama skills
- A still image
- Using mime, movement and gesture
- Speaking aloud in front of an audience
- Memorise a well-known story
(iii) Some pupils who can:
- Narrate a story
- Speak as a chorus
- Organise others
- Keep the teacher sane
(iv) A story
Any one will do (well almost) such as 'Cinderella'
(v) The secret formula for the Instant Assembly

Read on

A Still Image

In its simplest format it is when pupils create a picture which is frozen at a key moment. By 'reading' the picture, the audience gain part of the story and information about the characters. This is a very controlled drama teaching strategy.

In **a still image** make sure the pupils:
– stand still
– do not talk
– use space
– use their bodies
– use levels
– maintain eye contact
– breathe

Remember, every picture tells a story

Activating strategies

You can bring **a still image** to life in many different ways to deepen and extend the story – here are a few ideas:
– Through mime, movement and gesture
– Through slow-motion movement
– Through the thoughts of characters spoken aloud
– Through the dialogue between characters
– Through speaking as a chorus
– Through stepping out of the picture to make a comment to the audience
– Through stepping in to the picture to check on the action

THE SECRET FORMULA

One dose cures all assembly woes.

- Take a story e.g. Cinderella.
- Agree on a version of the tale.
- Divide the story into scenes.
- Make sure you have enough groups for at least one scene per group.
- Divide your class into groups.
- Give each group their scene.
  It helps if the running order of the scenes is written out and displayed in class.
- Tell each group to make a still image of their scene.
- Show the images in order
  Rehearse
  Redraft
  Redo
- Don't give up yet.
- Link each image by narration.
  The narrator could be the class teacher or a team of pupils.
  or
- Just do it in still pictures – quick; easy and effective!
- Give each group an activating strategy – a way of bringing a scene to life which is quick, simple and dramatically effective!
- Rehearse with narrator and see the pictures come to life.
- Give characters who appear in each scene, e.g. Cinderella, a piece of symbolic costume or a prop e.g. a broom.
  This can be passed from group. So, there are several Cinderellas and not one major star.
- Rehearse in the assembly space so they can get use to moving on and off the space.
- Try to create a one way traffic system, as in the diagram.

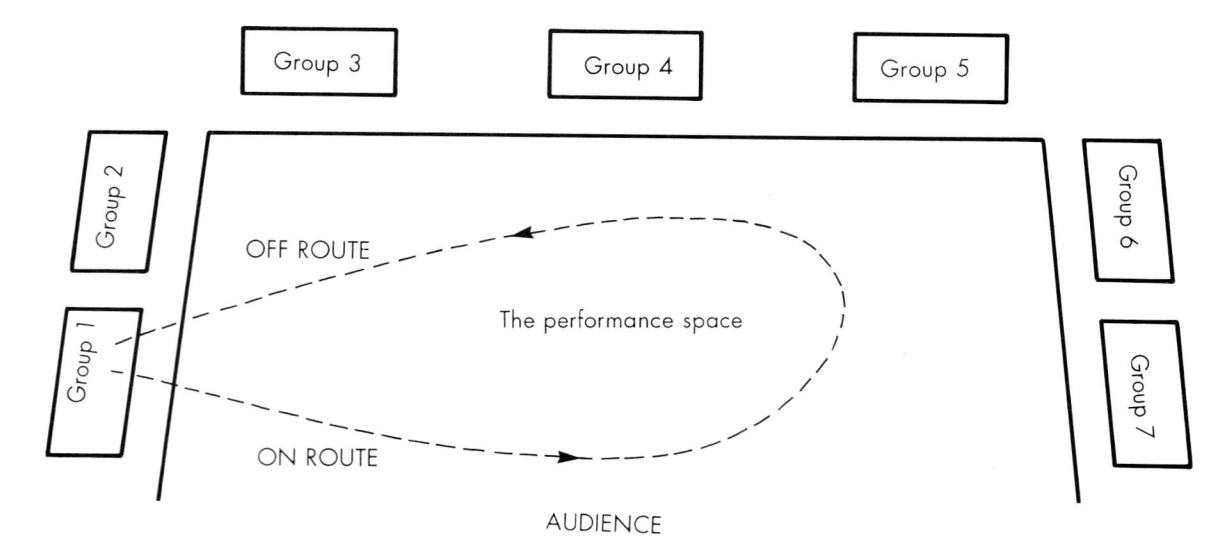

Group 1 get up, perform and return to their seating

- Seat the pupils in view of the audience on PE mats or a taped out area so they know their space.
- Keep props and costumes to a minimum.
- Enjoy the performance. It will be great.
- Video the pupils doing their story so they can see how well they did and how they could make it even better next time!
- In the example that follows, the story splits neatly into 12 scenes. This does not mean you need 12 groups! Do try to 'double up' on scenes. This gives your pupils lots to do and ensures that you have a workable number in your play.

THE STORY

This story is based on *Cinderella* by Fiona French published by O.U.P. 1989 (ISBN 0 1927 9 8413)

A possible running order

STILL IMAGE	ACTIVATING STRATEGIES
1. Cinderella meets her new stepmother and sisters.	Dialogue plus their personal thoughts spoken aloud.
2. Cinderella hard at work whilst her new family enjoy themselves.	Mime, movement and gesture Cinderella speaks her feelings to the house pets.
3. The invitation arrives.	Sounds – delight from all. Hoots of laughter at Cinderella.
4. Preparations at The Palace for the ball.	Chorus of comments from Palace workers.
5. Preparations at Cinderella's home.	Dialogue.
6. The fairy godmother arrives.	Slow motion movement and dialogue.
7. The animals become the coach*.	Thoughts spoken aloud.
8. The ball and the clock strikes midnight.	Movement and mime. Thoughts spoken aloud. Sounds
9. The slipper is found.	Thoughts and dialogue.
10. The search is on.	"Stepping out" to address the audience.
11. The shoe fits Cinderella.	Slow motion. Sounds.
12. They all live happily ever after.	Chorus.

* See Help point

HELP POINT

"Animals become the coach" — This technique is called 'physical imaging'. It is very simple, effective and does not require props. The characters simply turn themselves into an object using a frozen pose to start with and then they move in a manner appropriate to the object. In this sequence, the animals turn into Cinderella's coach, as in the diagram.

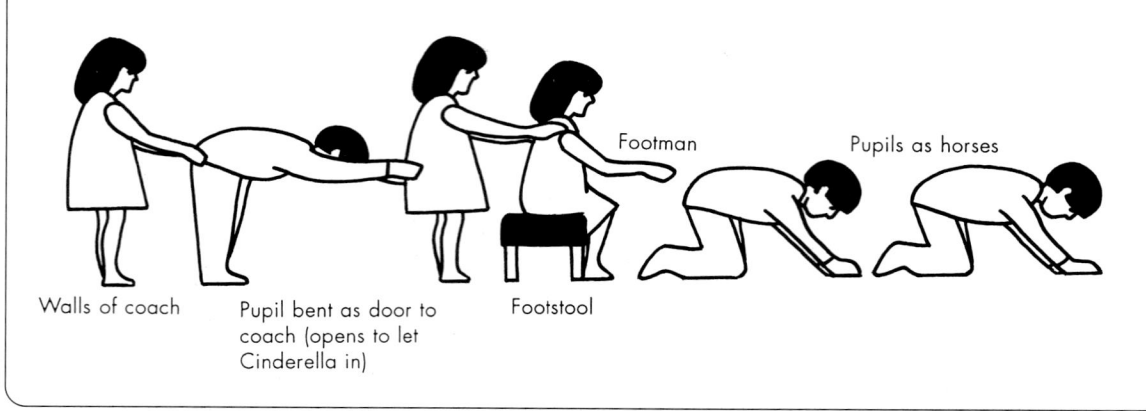

Walls of coach | Pupil bent as door to coach (opens to let Cinderella in) | Footstool | Footman | Pupils as horses

What will you do next time?
* **Beauty and The Beast.**
* **Aborigine Creation Myths.**
* **Anansi and the pot of gold.**

Any story will do, (well, almost).

This simple model is the basis of the drama approaches to be found in the projects. It is a model which works with pupils of all abilities and who have little or no experience of drama. The projects in this book aim to build on this model and to focus on some vital performance elements.

THE NATIVITY

INTRODUCTION

This is a whole school performance project which links the drama work to a term or half-termly topic. The emphasis is on the traditional Christian story of the birth of Jesus but the structure used here to bring the story to life can be applied to any story from any religion.

The structure of the project is based on simplicity. The end of autumn term event is often stressful and crammed into a few short weeks when staff and pupils are coming to the end of a long period of work. This project aims to take the stress out of organising a public event and put the fun back into it! It also emphasises the need to plan the performance as one part of a detailed topic so the play develops from class based research and work. It is *not* an unwelcome extra at the end of a long, tiring term but a natural evolving event and celebration to conclude a valuable term's work.

The end of term play can also link in with other curriculum subjects, as listed on page 17. Performance also provides a rich learning environment for drama itself. A table covering the learning areas for both key stages is on page 18 under *The Dramatic Curriculum*.

This project gives you a detailed plan of a story and characters of *The Animals Nativity* – the story and characters are given in depth. The *Running Order* of the performance is offered as a guide. Do add more according to the size of your class or school.

Each scene is then given an extended profile to give you the flavour of the event. There is no script. The scenes will be developed through basic improvisation techniques which can be done in class or in hall time. Let the pupils develop the scene – just give them the framework. Their ideas are usually better than the teachers! As they rehearse, they'll redraft until it becomes a polished piece of improvisation. A script may evolve as older pupils add more to the scenes or take on a major linking role to the play as a whole. It gives a wonderful purpose for writing. Finally, there are some *Production Techniques* on how to shape the event in your school or place of worship plus a few hints on organisation and keeping sane.

> **TIP**
> Don't forget – go back to the 'Instant Assembly Model' if you get stuck and begin with the basic building block of drama work: the Still Image.

Involving *every* child in a major event is a marvellous experience for all and it is one which they will never forget. It is a great platform for learning about other religions and cultures and a great opportunity to develop performing skills within a tried, tested and successful formula.

THE SUBJECT MATTER

Religious festivals provide an excellent vehicle for performance work in schools. By exploring these events through drama pupils are able to:

- Gain knowledge and understanding about other cultures in their school and community.
- Draw upon local community experts who can bring their specialist knowledge to enhance and deepen the pupils' work.
- Regenerate interest in well-known and sometimes worn-out stories such as the Christian festival of The Nativity

By exploring these festivals through performance based drama the pupils can resource their work through topic-based research.

Many festivals require specialised dances or traditional musical instruments. By exploring them through performance the pupils gain a broad knowledge of the artistic culture and heritage of these festivals.

Some festivals which lead themselves easily to performance work are:

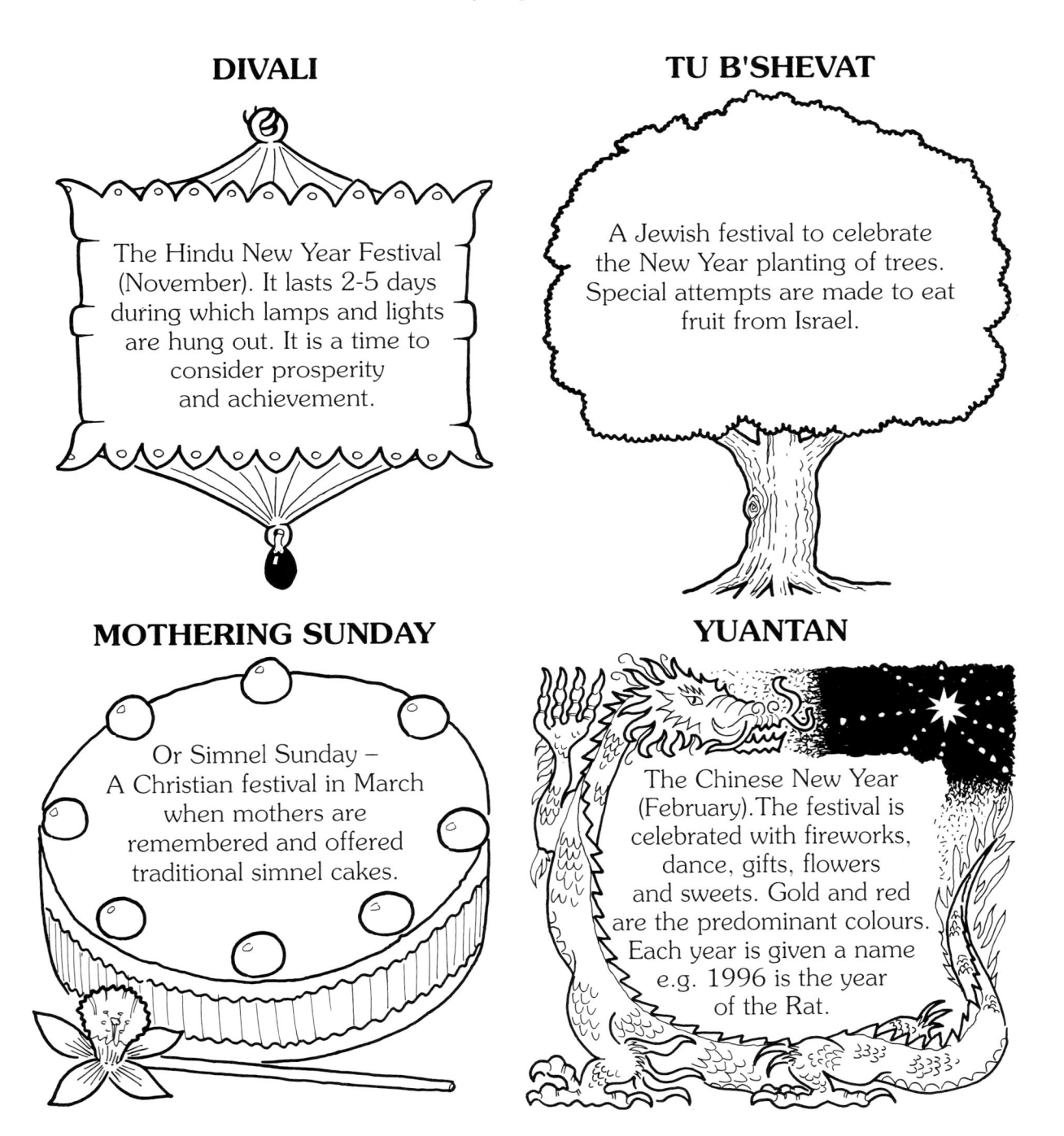

DIVALI

The Hindu New Year Festival (November). It lasts 2-5 days during which lamps and lights are hung out. It is a time to consider prosperity and achievement.

TU B'SHEVAT

A Jewish festival to celebrate the New Year planting of trees. Special attempts are made to eat fruit from Israel.

MOTHERING SUNDAY

Or Simnel Sunday –
A Christian festival in March when mothers are remembered and offered traditional simnel cakes.

YUANTAN

The Chinese New Year (February). The festival is celebrated with fireworks, dance, gifts, flowers and sweets. Gold and red are the predominant colours. Each year is given a name e.g. 1996 is the year of the Rat.

The performing platform

The Nativity project explores the traditional Christian festival of the birth of Jesus.

The Nativity project can:

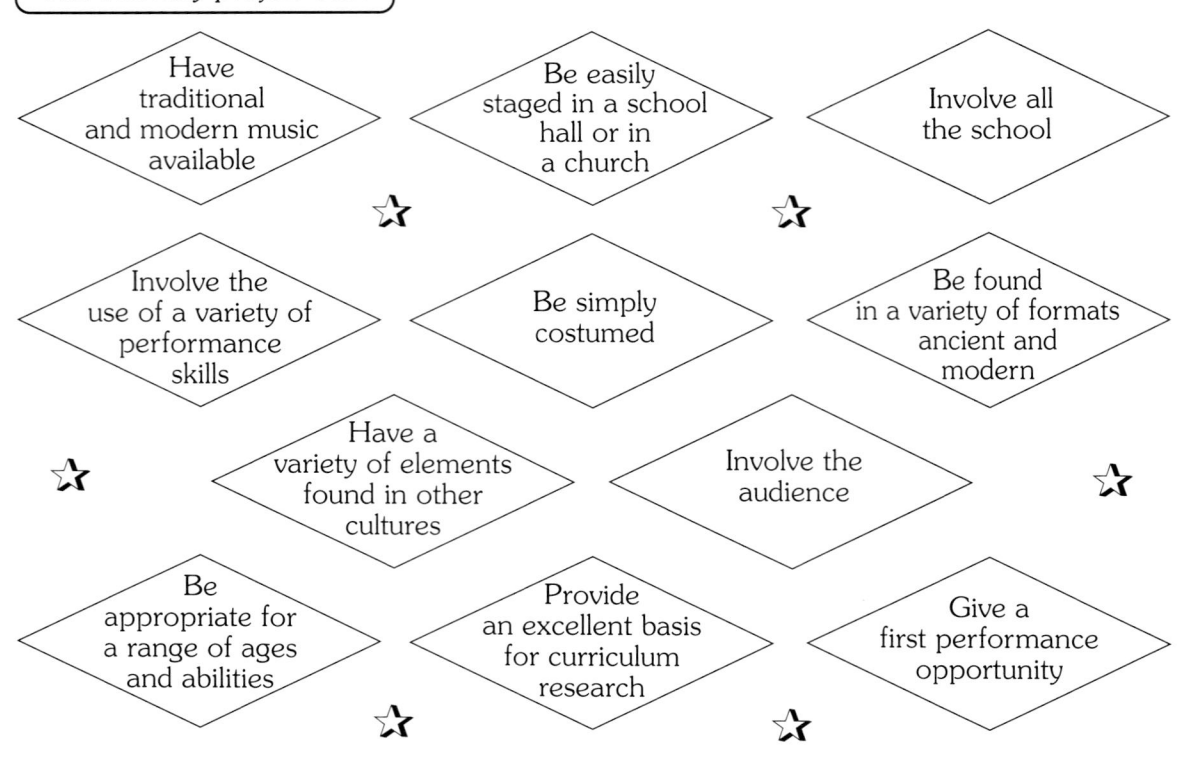

- Have traditional and modern music available
- Be easily staged in a school hall or in a church
- Involve all the school
- Involve the use of a variety of performance skills
- Be simply costumed
- Be found in a variety of formats ancient and modern
- Have a variety of elements found in other cultures
- Involve the audience
- Be appropriate for a range of ages and abilities
- Provide an excellent basis for curriculum research
- Give a first performance opportunity

CURRICULUM LINKS

Try not to see this story as an isolated event which happens once a year in December. If properly planned and resourced it can provide a rich area of study for at least half a term and can deliver a range of required subjects.

For example:

HISTORY	KS 1 :	Events which have been remembered and commemorated by succeeding generations e.g. religious festivals
	KS 2 :	Life under the Romans e.g. invaders and settlers
GEOGRAPHY	KS 1 :	A contrasting locality
	KS 2 :	Places and themes
SCIENCE	KS 1 :	Materials; physical processes
	KS 2 :	Growth and reproduction; Earth and beyond
MUSIC	KS 1 :	Singing; musical effects; music from different times and places
	KS 2 :	Rhythmic and melodic ideas music reflecting time and place
ENGLISH	KS 1 :	Developing pupils' speech and communications with others in formal situations e.g. assemblies; learning some rhymes and poetry by heart
	KS 2 :	Widening drama activities e.g. writing a script for performance variety of reading texts

These are just a few recommended suggestions. A wide range of work across the school could be stimulated by this drama project.

The class-based work jogs alongside the performing work in a mutually supportive relationship based on research, resources, rigours, active learning and enjoyment.

Planning your nativity will give you a complete whole school topic.

Some further ideas

DRAMA
- Narrative sequence
- Variety of roles
- Script writing
- Costume
- Props
- Masks
- Puppets
- Teacher in role

R.E.
- Exploring Christian traditions
- The bible stories
- Christian concepts e.g. love

LANGUAGE
- Storytelling technique
- Oral traditions
- Researching different versions
- Christmas cards
  Calenders
  Advent calendars
- Film/TV portrayals
- Creating their own version

MUSIC
- Carols
- Music of the time
- Instruments of the time
- Soundscapes of the stable

MATHS
- Timelines
- Calendars
- Number work e.g. 3
- A census

SCIENCE
- Stars and the heavens
- Light and dark
- Human life cycle
- Animal welfare

HISTORY
- Timelines
- Census
- Life under the Romans
- How they used to live
- Costume
- Christmas trees

DANCE
- Dances of tradition
- Traditional festivals
- Gestures

GEOGRAPHY
- Journeys
- Map
- Climate
- Where in the world
- People
- Work and play

TECHNOLOGY
- Pop up Christmas cards
- A baby carrier model
- Advent crowns
- The gift box

ART
- The work of artists in representing the story
- Stamps
- Wrapping paper
- Cards
- Objects for a Christmas tree

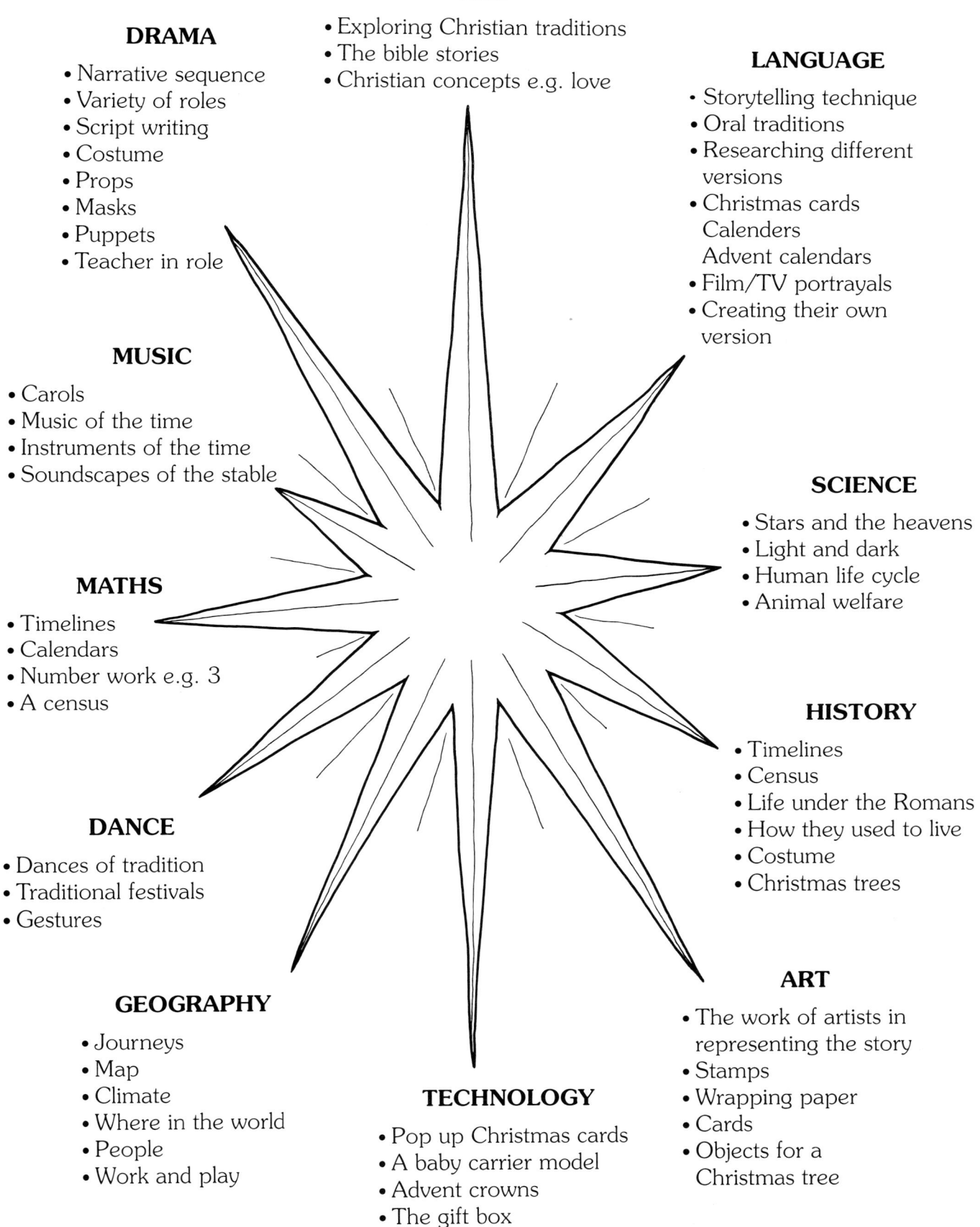

THE DRAMATIC CURRICULUM

By performing your version of the nativity you will be using a range of drama activities. The pupils learn the skills that enable them to create a positive performing experience. Here are some aspects of drama that this project covers.

	Key Stage 1	**Key Stage 2**
MAKING	Telling a story through a play Pretending to be someone else Remembering their part	Tell a story through a play using same drama conventions e.g. thought tracking Create a character using words and movement appropriately Improvise their ideas and shape into a finished product
PERFORMING	Show the play to an audience Wear a costume Speak words aloud Sing Learn to get on and offstage efficiently	Show the play to an audience Design and make a costume or prop, and use them appropriately Use simple lighting and settings
RESPONDING	Talk about their part in the play See other classes perform Watch a video of their work	Talk about their part in the play and how they would make it better Relate their performance to others they may have seen out of school

HOW TO START

- Tell the pupils the story. Use a range of resources from non-fiction to fiction.
- Find out their versions of the story. What is their understanding of the events?
- Try writing the story with different audiences in mind.
    - e.g. as a bedtime story
    - as a letter from King Herod to a neighbouring King
    - as a news report
    - as a diary entry by Joseph
- It is important to start from the pupils' viewpoint
- Then you can add further resources
- Research the various biblical versions of the story
    - Matthew 1 vv. 18-24 The angel foretells the birth
    - Luke 1 vv. 26-33
    - Luke 2 vv. 1-7 The journey and the birth
    - Luke 2 vv. 8-20 The shepherds
    - Matthew 2 vv. 1-12 The three wise men
    - Matthew 2 vv. 13-23 The flight to Egypt
- Having got the evidence, look at other sources – there are many.

Some examples are:
   The Christmas Story – Brian Wildsmith
   Away in a Manger – Sara Hayes
   Christmas in the Stable – Astrid Lindgren

or

- Create your own idea
    * The story through the eyes of people from other cultures
    * The story through the eyes of creatures from another planet
    * The story through the eyes of children from around the world
    * The story through the eyes of the animals in the stable
    * The story through the eyes of Joseph or Mary or the angels

The combinations are endless but which ever route you take, follow the structure laid out in Instant Assembly Model as your starting point and build from there.

You can have a script but do build this from improvisational work that the pupils complete. It is then their words in the script and not an adult-only style. This makes for a more meaningful production.

The animal's nativity

This idea has been used in large and small primary schools where every pupil has been involved. It has been performed in churches, halls and vestrys so it is very flexible. Each class takes one scene and works on it with the class teacher during drama/hall time.

Songs are rehearsed during music or assembly time. Costumes and props are made as part of the class topic. The scenes are enhanced by class projects or topic work which help the pupils to focus on the story. Drama brings their class work to life.

Each class performs their scene in turn, with changeovers linked by songs. Everyone appears in the final scene either in the tableau or as a procession moving around the hall or church so every child receives applause.

The drama and the other subject areas work together to support, resource, inform and achieve a wonderful whole school topic.

Pupils make a procession around the scene in the final tableau.

CREATING THE STORY

Here is an example of how to develop one idea.

● Scenario

The traditional nativity story told through the eyes of the animals in the stable where Jesus is born.

● Aims of the project

- To perform a play to an audience of parents and friends.
- To involve all the pupils in the school.
- To costume and stage the event simply and cheaply.
- To perform it in the school hall.
- To link the play to the 'Celebrations' topic.
- To keep the whole project manageable by delegation.

● Action points

- Create enough scenes for at least one per class.
- Each scene is devised through spontaneous improvisation, rehearsing until it becomes a polished piece.
- Each class could use Instant Assembly Model.
- You will need to add songs and dances.
- Narrator, e.g. The Angels, link the scenes and carry the story.
- Develop the script from the pupils' work. Get them to note down by hand or on a word processor.
- Each class does at least one scene so the class teacher is the director (and referee).
- Have regular meetings with colleagues to keep up to date.
- Sort out hall time.
- Sort out an approach to costume.

But first...the storyline.

● The main characters

HUMANS	ANIMALS
• Mary • Joseph • Baby Jesus • Shepherds • Three Wise Men • Angels • Market Traders • Herod • Workers at Herod's palace • Children of the world	• The old donkey • 3 camels • Oxen • Lambs • Birds of peace • Naughty rats

RUNNING ORDER

Scene 1
The main tableau which begins and ends the play is in the stable with all the animals present.
The angels as narrators set the scene and set up the 'Flashback' structure
e.g. Angel 1: "How did all these animals get here?"
   Angel 2: "I bet they all have a story to tell"
   Angel 3: "Let's go back in time and hear how they came to be in this stable at this important time"

LINK WITH A CAROL

This allows pupils to get on and off stage effectively.

Scene 2
The Donkey's Tale

Scene 3
The angels introduce the naughty rats and set their quest which is that they must deliver a special message wrapped on a scroll to the new King whom they'll find in a stable surrounded by animals.

LINK WITH A CAROL

Scene 4
The narrators introduce the next scene.

Scene 5   The Camel's Tale

LINK WITH A CAROL

Scene 6
The narrators introduce the next scene.

Scene 7
The rats interrupt the narrators

Scene 8
The Oxen's Tale

LINK WITH A CAROL

Scene 9
Narrators introduce the next scene.

Scene 10   The Lamb's Tale

Scene 11
The rats pester the narrators.

LINK WITH A CAROL

Scene 12
The Birds of Peace Tale

Scene 13
Rats chase the birds away and interact with the audience.

Scene 14
Narrators introduce The Children of the World.

LINK WITH A CAROL

Scene15
All join the final tableau.

Scene 16
Final tableau plus:
The rats read their message
The narrators finish the story

END ON A CAROL

– all pupils can then slowly walk around the stage singing and accepting applause.

Extending the story

THE DONKEY'S TALE

The scene is set in a busy stable in Nazareth. There are horses, donkeys, stable workers, blacksmiths, grooms at work (even a vet?)

Each group takes a turn to step out of the action to tell the audience about their job; their feelings and the preparations for the long journey to Bethlehem to be taxed. Whilst the actors speak aloud, the other performers fall silent and freeze. When the actors finish their piece, the stables leap back into a lively, noisy setting

Each group makes a comment about the old donkey who is stabled in the corner – unwanted, unkempt and unloved.

The old donkey can tell her story: a sad story of mistreatment and pain.

Into the busy stable come Mary and Joseph wanting to hire a donkey.

The stable owner, a garrulous character who would sell anything, takes his prospective customers on a tour.

He tries to sell them everything.

They reject all offers until they come across the old donkey.

To everyone's amazement, they settle on the old donkey. The stable owner faints from shock.

Mary and Joseph exit with a spritely old donkey.

THE CAMEL'S TALE

The scene is set at the starting point of the camel train which will lead the three wise men to the stable.

There are three main camels – these ones will carry the wine men.

They are full of self importance.

Three smaller camels will carry the servants to the wine men.

Then come the working camels who have to carry the luggage and supplies.

They are a grumbly bunch and mutter about overwork, low pay and no action from their union.

Each main camel has a family they are leaving behind. The scene develops this relationship and the audience can gain an insight into the camels' feelings.

The smaller camels are given strict instructions on behaviour by their parents who remain at home.

The luggage camels moan a lot!

The three wise men and servants enter carrying their gifts of gold, frankincense and myrrh.

The audience can hear about their gift, their importance and the reason for the journey.

The cue to set off is the appearance of the Star, their guiding light (a slide projected onto the ceiling or wall).

As they move off, we hear the thoughts of the camels and their passengers.

TIP

> Use half masks for each camel so we can hear their speeches clearly. See 'Serpent King' project page 73 for mask making ideas.

THE OXENS' TALE

The scene is set in a busy market place in Bethlehem; lots of stalls, lots of market sellers and shoppers, thieves, dealers and auctioneers.

The scene starts with pupils in position, frozen. On a given cue, the market bursts into life.

Try to orchestrate each market stall so that the audience can hear the market cries clearly.

Give each group a number and then they can go in order. A bell can be the signal for the changeover. Whilst one group does its piece, the other market folk are silent but keep miming.

e.g. All in unison)
    Stall one   )
    Bell   ) This gives the
    All   ) sequence a
    Bell   ) rhythm for
    Stall two   ) the choral
    Bell   ) speaking
    All   )
    Bell   )
    Stall three etc.)

Enter a herd of oxen arriving for an auction.

The market halts as people gather for the auction.

An auctioneer steps up onto the box.

An auction takes place.

The best oxen are sold. What remains are an ox and two calves. Their mother is sold off.

These oxen step out of the action and speak their thoughts.

An innkeeper arrives late and offers to buy these leftover oxen. He herds them off to an old stable muttering about oxtail soup and roast dinners!

They are led to a stable.

THE LAMBS' TALE

On the hills overlooking Bethlehem, groups of shepherds huddle around small fires, sharing wine and stories.

One group shares a story about a prophecy of the birth of a new King.

They have finished their work as night falls. Gentle songs are sung; a game of stones takes place and dancing occurs. Across the stage, frozen whilst the shepherds perform, is a group of lambs and sheep.

The lambs are playing, getting naughtier and bolder as they taunt their elders.

The older sheep wander off to new pastures, leaving the lambs to follow.

The lambs decide to play with the shepherds but are interrupted by the arrival of the Angels who relate the story to the ensemble.

The lambs rush to tell their elders who do not believe them and pour scorn on the story.

The lambs follow the shepherds to the stable.

THE BIRDS OF PEACE TALE

This scene takes place in Herod's palace where the workers are preparing for a great banquet.

There are cooks, cleaners, maids, gardeners all busy with their work.

The birds of peace are in a cage awaiting their owners who are the court entertainers.

Whilst the workers freeze in action, we hear about the miserable life of these birds. They long to escape.

A small sparrow arrives and hears their story. She has heard of the birth of a new King and is on her way to the place but needs some food and rest. She waits by the cage.

Enter Herod and his entourage ready for a banquet and entertainment.

His maître d'hôte hosts the event and, in the style of a fashion show, commentates on each dish of food as it arrives.

There is a dance display.

Then, the entertainers arrive.

They are incompetent and things go wrong.

The muddle is worsened as people try to help. Herod is angry and in the tussle, the cage is knocked over and the birds of peace escape, led by the sparrow.

To make matters worse, the three Kings arrive, searching for a new King.

Herod's anger is now complete.

Everyone is dismissed and Herod is left to tell the audience his cruel plan.

> **TIP**
> If you intend to share parts, such as those of the wise men, then make sure that the costumes are the same or have similar elements e.g. a turban or crown to give continuity for the audience.

THE CHILDREN OF THE WORLD

This scene is an excellent vehicle for including your pre-school group and/or your reception classes.

Their task is to decide on a present for the new baby.

The gift could represent the country they came from.

Using mime, they wrap their gift and each group, in chorus, tells the audience their choice.

e.g. a woolly hat to keep him warm.
a shell so he can hear the sea.
some beads on a string so he can learn to count.
a cuddly koala to keep him safe at night.

They exit with gifts to reappear in the final tableau.

TIP

> If you are performing in the evening, make sure these pupils do their piece early on in the play so they can be taken home before it gets too late. Their gifts can be on stage ready in the tableau.
>
> If you have a number of classes, let one class only perform each night so they all have a turn but are not tired out by a series of late nights.

THE NAUGHTY RATS

The rats are a useful linking device and a way of using more able pupils who would benefit from this extension work.

The rats have an important message to deliver to the stable. It is in a smart scroll, and was left at the entrance to their home.

They interrupt the narrators, appear in the scenes, engage the audience, are seen during scene changeovers as they set about finding directions to the stable.

They can appear and engage in dialogue or they can run, in silence, miming, through a scene.

They eventually arrive at the stable and are welcomed by Mary and Joseph.

They are asked to read out the message which consists of a seasonal greeting to end the play.

The rats can also be useful in helping out in scenes which use younger pupils e.g. they could help the Children of the World or cause havoc in Herod's palace. They can also act as prompts if pupils forget words or as leaders to lead pupils off stage.

They could, also lead the audience in carol singing!

THE FINAL TABLEAU

You need all the main players on stage. If you are stuck for space, choose a representative number e.g. 2 lambs from the group.

If you have a large stage area get all the characters on.

The gifts from Children of the World can be arranged around the crib. Use a suitable doll to represent baby Jesus.

The rest of the cast can parade around the stage area singing the final carol. Keep them moving on stage and then exit back to classrooms.

Use aisles, exits and entrances but keep the flow of pupils moving to ensure a hasty exit if required.

HELP POINT

> With a large cast, ensure that they are based in a classroom or area in their scene groups. A member of staff will be in charge of moving each group into an area which is set aside for the next scene. This is a silent waiting area. The class performs and then exits to their base.
>
> The next scene group are ready in the foyer or backstage awaiting their cue to move from this special waiting area.
>
> It will mean that pupils will not see the final version. Make sure one dress rehearsal is set aside for pupils to stay in the hall after their scene so they do get a view of the whole performance.

PRODUCTION TECHNIQUES

Costumes

Keep it simple

Use half masks; gloves; tails made from wool and coat hangers;
T.shirts/jumpers; leggings and/or tights.
Decide on colours for each scene.
e.g. Herod's palace is blue and silver
       The market is yellow and green
       The shepherds are white, blue and purple
       The camel train are shades of brown
Try to avoid tea towels, dressing gowns and trainers.

Staging

To be effective: *Keep it simple.* You do not need huge sets of complex scenery and complicated lighting effects for a successful performance. The simpler the better and cheaper too!

Once you have decided on your performance space, you need to choose the best shape of stage for the production. Do not forget your audience. They need to see as much as possible whilst sitting comfortably. Simple rosta blocks and flexible staging systems are highly useful and can be made to fit any space. Here are a few ideas for staging. *See* the diagrams on staging positions on the next page.

1. AUDIENCE
Raise the seating so they look down on the action or vice versa. Try not to have performers and audience on the same level. Ensure performers can be seen from all angles. It stops anxious parents bobbing up and down or standing in aisles!

2. PERFORMERS
It can be effective to have performers seated in full view of audience. They enter and exit the performance as rehearsed but can also be active viewers too. This helps backstage policing!

3. ENTRANCE & EXITS
Be flexible. Have plenty of options so the flow of the performance is not interrupted whilst the performers queue up to leave the stage.

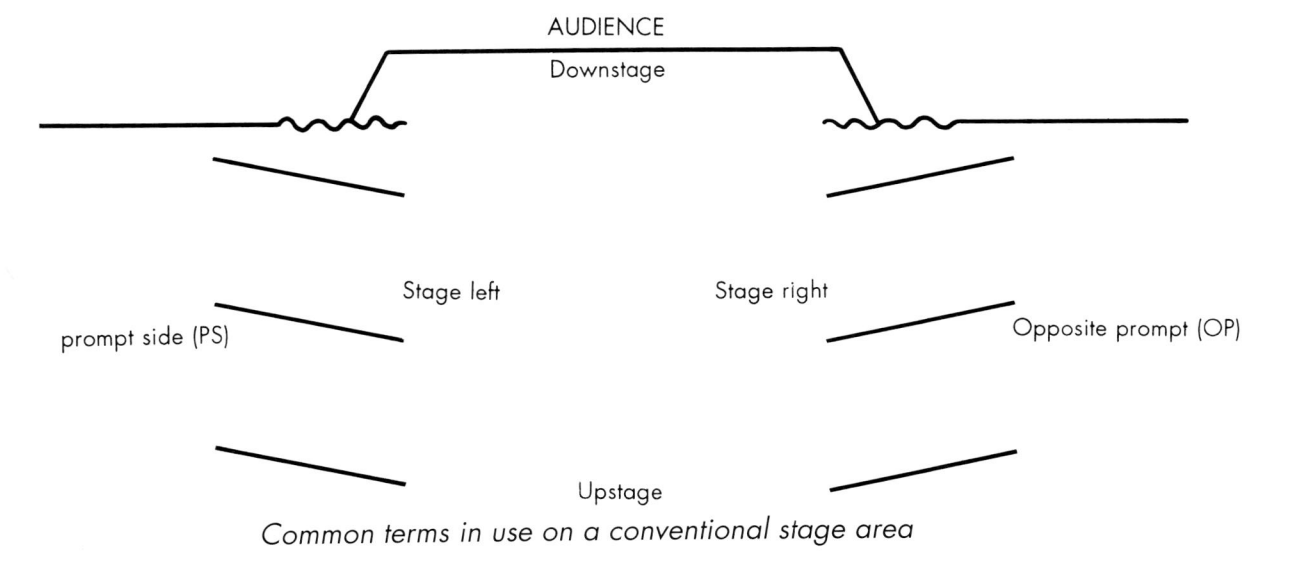

AUDIENCE

Downstage

Stage left   Stage right

prompt side (PS)   Opposite prompt (OP)

Upstage

Common terms in use on a conventional stage area

STAGING POSITIONS

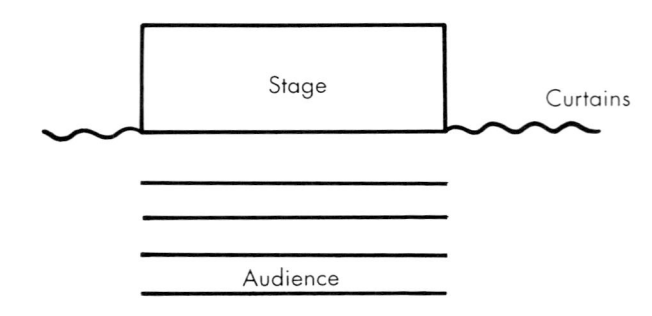

END ON
Raised stage, audience seated in rows below. Use rosta blocks to build out from stage. Curtains hide backstage areas. If there are no curtains, improvise with screens. Traditional school hall style.

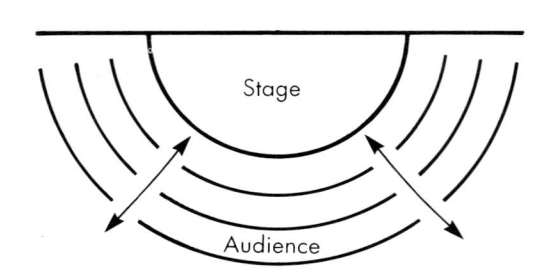

GREEK
1/2 circle stage.
Audience seated in raised curves looking down on action. Aisles are entrances and exits. Outdoor theatre for school grounds.

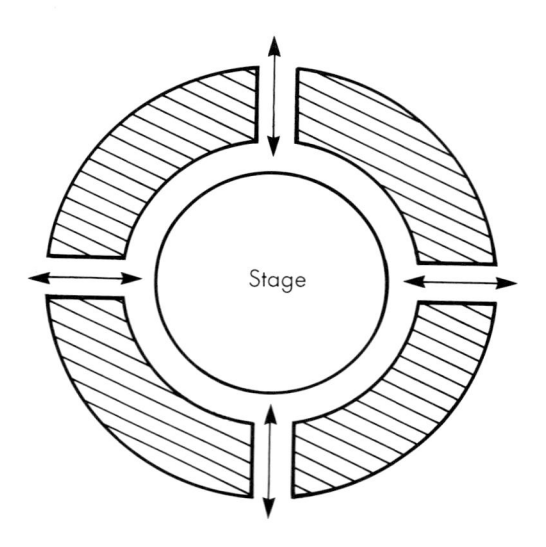

IN THE ROUND
Audience and performers can be on same level. Raise back seats for good sight lines.
Four routes on and off stage.
Small studio style or big gym space.

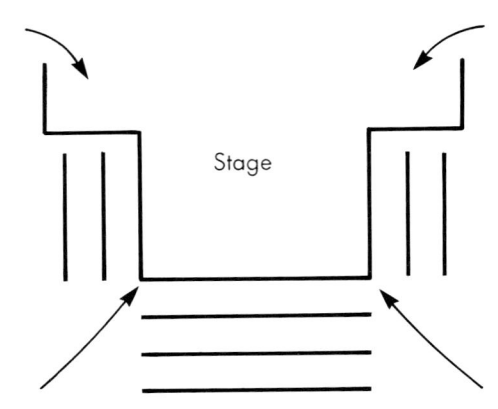

THRUST
Raised stage – audience on lower level on 3 sides.
Fashion show style and Elizabethan style too!

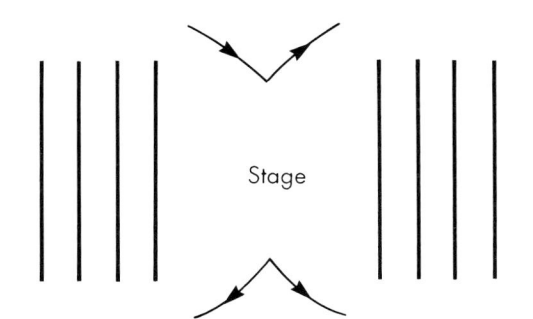

AVENUE
Audience raised on either side of performance space.
Good shape for dance and musical shows.

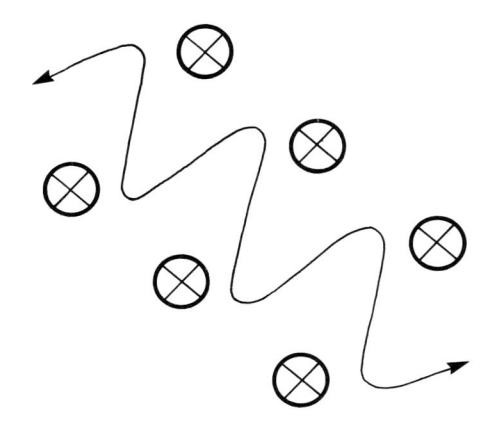

PROMENADE
Audience walk to performance spaces and watch. Spaces could be classroom venues or special spaces in the hall!
Medieval style: useful for nativity events.

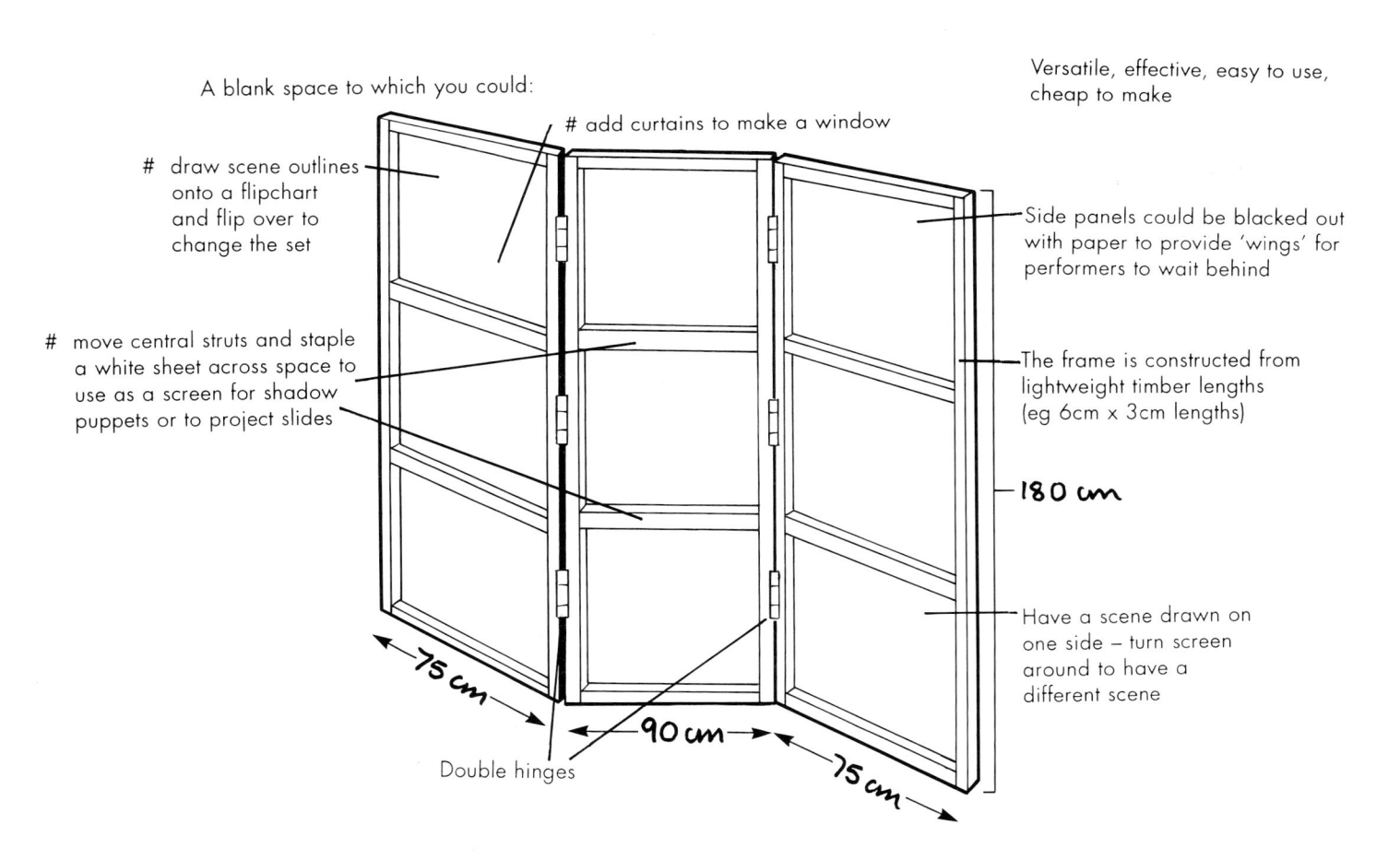

A blank space to which you could:

add curtains to make a window

draw scene outlines onto a flipchart and flip over to change the set

move central struts and staple a white sheet across space to use as a screen for shadow puppets or to project slides

Versatile, effective, easy to use, cheap to make

Side panels could be blacked out with paper to provide 'wings' for performers to wait behind

The frame is constructed from lightweight timber lengths (eg 6cm x 3cm lengths)

180 cm

Have a scene drawn on one side – turn screen around to have a different scene

75 cm

90 cm

75 cm

Double hinges

Stage equipment: a drama screen

> **HELP POINT**
>
> Linking it all together.
>
> - Each class devises and rehearses in their own time — in class time or in hall time.
> - Each class teacher is responsible for their scene, costumes and props.
> - One teacher needs overall responsibility to pull it all together and work on
>   - narrators
>   - rats
>   - linking carols
>   - backstage area
>   - seating
>   - entrances and exits
> - Try to rehearse scenes together
>
>   e.g. Monday scenes 1, 2 & 3
>   Tuesday scenes 1, 2 & 3 plus rats and narrators
>   Wednesday scenes 3, 4, 5 etc
>   so there begins to be continuity and purpose.
> - Devise a schedule
> - Have two runthroughs without costume
> - Have two dress rehearsals — one with pupils as audience and one with pupils backstage.
> - Have singing rehearsals for the carols.
> - Have one rehearsal for entrances and exit training.
> - Video the final dress rehearsal in full light so it records well.
> - Draw up contingency plans in case main characters fall sick.

CONCLUSION

The essential element of this project is simplicity.

The purpose of this performance project is to allow the whole school to become involved and share the work which an audience will then see.

The content of each scene will be appropriate to the needs, skills and interests of each class. The project involves sharing, through simple performance techniques of a well known story. It is essential that the performance derives from a class-based topic so pupils develop a rounded picture of these historical events to balance the imaginative elements of the story.

This is tried and tested material and has worked successfully with a variety of pupils, places and with teachers whose performance experience ranged from non-existent to professional level. So, give it a try and enjoy the results.

THE 'DEAR GREENPEACE' PROJECT

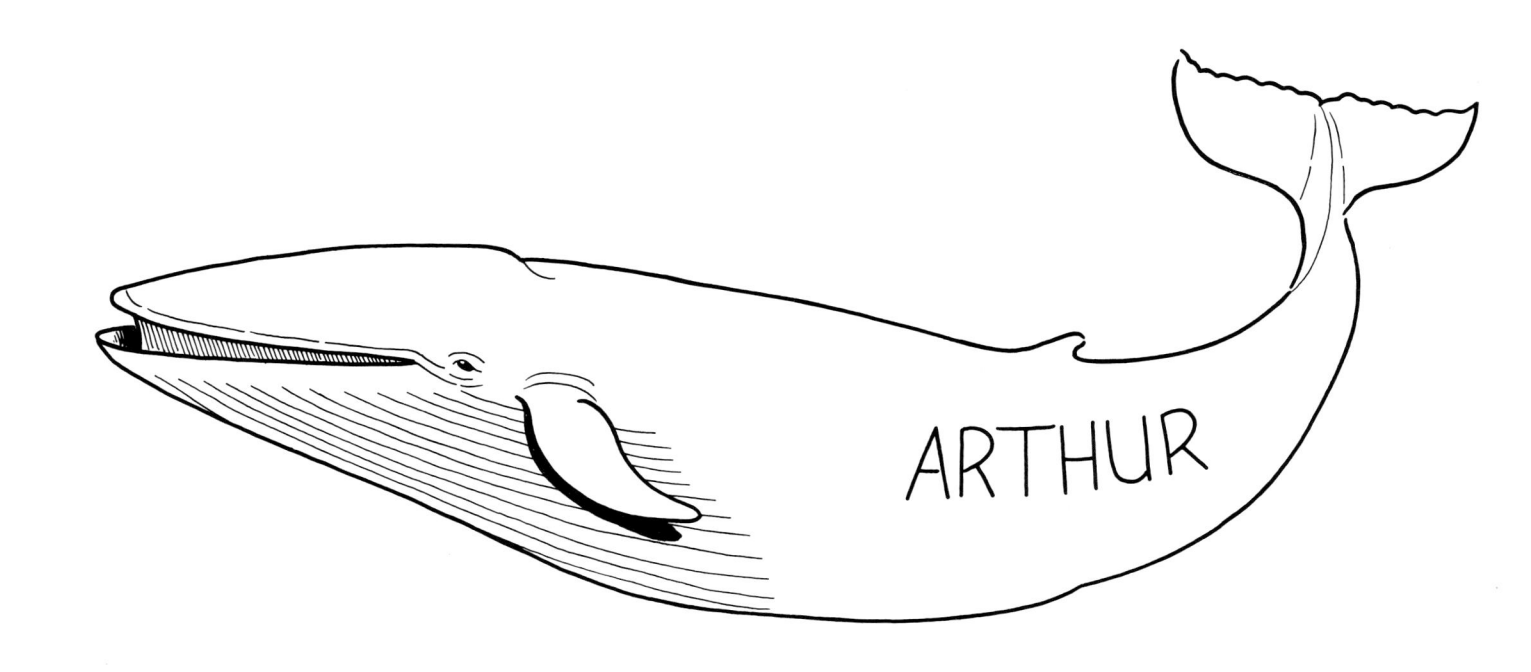

INTRODUCTION

This performance project is very different from *The Animals' Nativity*, being more complex and demanding. It is suited to years 5 and 6.

This delightful children's story has an environmental focus. It is written in the form of short letters between Emily, the heroine and the environmental pressure group Greenpeace. The exchange of letters focus on Emily and Arthur, a blue whale who lives in her pond!

It is a challenging story to turn into a performance piece because:

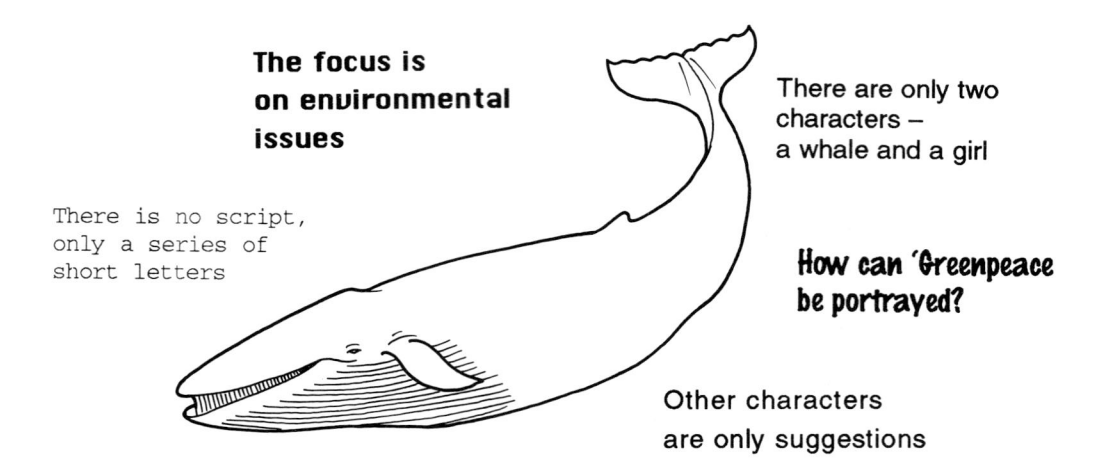

The focus is on environmental issues

There is no script, only a series of short letters

There are only two characters – a whale and a girl

How can 'Greenpeace be portrayed?

Other characters are only suggestions

The whole piece is based upon the premise that each scene will be improvised and developed into a polished final piece. The story, though simple, is challenging because it leaves a lot to the imagination. This demands a great deal of creative development in order to make the piece work. It is also a piece of drama that works with very few props or costumes but requires careful lighting. Whereas with The Nativity Project, the audience will have some knowledge of the story and so can fill in any gaps, this story will probably be unknown and thus demands careful narrative structure in order to make sense.

So it is a demanding and challenging piece which is successful with pupils who have got performing experience and who are able to develop work from the minimal stimuli.

As with all the projects, there is a strong link to the whole curriculum. The project fits neatly into environmental topics. Some ideas are given for you to develop in *Cross Curricular Links*.

Whilst this project has been successful with pupils from years 5 and 6, it could be attempted with younger pupils with some major adjustments, shown in the section *Dramatic Curriculum*. With both key stages, a rich drama curriculum is exploited throughout this project.

A brief synopsis is given in *Creating the Story*. It is enhanced by details of the characters which need to be created in order for the play to make sense. Ideas for developing the 'Greenpeace' characters are offered. All of which feeds into a proposed running order for the project. Again, each scene is given further extended coverage to give a picture of the possible contents. Do add, amend or precis as required.

Staging ideas are offered along with detailed explanations of stage lighting – the mechanics, lanterns and approaches and ideas for sound in *Staging the Event*. Also in this section health and safety issues are covered as well as ideas for getting equipment without incurring too much cost.

This project aims to encourage you to try to turn challenging material into exciting performance projects for pupils of all abilities. Any text can be used – this is one example. It demands creative team work to make it successful. It also provides a rich learning resource about a vital cross curricular theme as well as aspects of the drama curriculum such as staging, lighting and sound. These will attract pupils who do not wish to perform but who want to be part of the production team.

TECHNOLOGY
- Design a whale for the production
- Materials needed
- Design plan
- Making
- Testing
- Evaluation

DANCE
- Representing aspects of story or characters through movement

SCIENCE
- The life cycle of a blue whale
- Evolution
- Mammals
- Human influences
- Environmental

GEOGRAPHY
- Seas and oceans
- Protecting and managing environment
- Climate
- Use and misuse of natural resources
- Maps
- Field studies e.g. beaches
- Cultural use of whales/whaling trade

PERSONAL, SOCIAL EDUCATION
- Caring
- Listening
- Belief in your ideas

MUSIC
- Sounds of ocean creatures
- composing whale songs
- recording

ART
- Recording ideas, design
- Different materials e.g. 3D representation of the whale in the pond
- Representations of whales with different artists and craftworkers

DRAMA
- Lighting
- Staging
- Sound

ENGLISH
- Letter writing to a specific audience
- Scriptwork
- Whale stories in literature from European, North American and Asian culture

THE DRAMATIC CURRICULUM

This story can be used to support the delivery of several aspects of the dramatic curriculum.

	Key Stage 1	Key Stage 2
MAKING	Making a play from a story Sharing a story with others Playing different parts in a pretend	Making a play from a story incorporating dramatic conventions e.g. stepping out of the action; voices off Playing different parts including inanimate objects
PERFORMING	Acting out the story Using mime and words to play a part in a play	Performing in an ensemble Learning lines or remembering a part Using simple lighting and sound techniques Working with props they have made
RESPONDING	Talking about the play they have been in and how it felt	Talking about the play and its relationship to the environmental issues

CREATING THE STORY

- The play of the book
- Characters
- Staging
- Lighting
- Sound
- Making the whale

THE STORY

A brief synopsis

The story concerns Emily, a young girl who begins to write letters to the environmental pressure group *Greenpeace* about a blue whale who is living in the garden pond!

Greenpeace dutifully respond, gently attempting to persuade Emily that she has made a mistake and the whale is all in her imagination.

Emily will not be put off and she maintains her correspondence, requesting information on diet, watery environment and migration patterns.

Greenpeace respond, their tone becoming more exasperated as they try to persuade Emily that a blue whale could not possibly survive in a domestic pond!

Emily persists. She is, after all, right. One night, Arthur the blue whale, disappears and re-appears on a beach about to swim off to the distant ocean. They say their farewells.

Emily writes a final note to Greenpeace just to confirm her findings.

It is a charming tale about a child's belief in her truthful findings and the scepticism of a large, faceless organisation.

Having read the story, it is time to set about turning it into a performance piece – not for two characters but a class of at least thirty five pupils!

All it needs is a little ingenuity, imagination and planning.

The characters

Emily   (1)

Arthur, the whale   (3)

Greenpeace – an office
of several people   (6)

OTHERS

Emily's family   – Dad
                 – Mum
                 – Baby brother (3)

Emily's school
(friends & teacher)   (10)

The postman/woman   (1)

Neighbours : several   (6)

People on the beach: several   (5)

TOTAL =   35

So all one class can be involved!

The performing platform

SCENES
The story suggests seven scenes
At home 5 possible scenes
- In the garden and pond
- In Emily's bedroom
- At the breakfast table
- By the letterbox in the hall
- In the sitting room

plus
- At school
- At the seaside

Not all of this need be staged. At the same time more could be added to enhance the story. Having got the bare outline, it is now time to build in extensions to the story, add scenes and develop characters.

HELP POINT

The main area to develop is 'The Greenpeace Office'. This can be performed in two possible ways.

1) Five or six people working in a busy office. They all contribute to the discussions of the letters and the content of the responses.
Use improvisation to develop the characters, their relationships and their roles in the office.
This approach gives scope for using a number of pupils — some in non-speaking roles.

2) One character plays 'Greenpeace':
The letters are read onto tape and played back during the appropriate scenes.
The character sits at a desk and mimes as the voice is played back.
This is a more stylised and theatrical approach.
It is useful if you are doing the play with a small cast as part of a drama club.

THE RUNNING ORDER

This section offers you a running order based on successful performances of this project.
There is
(i) A list of titles of each scene.
(ii) An extended description of each scene to help give you a picture of the contents.

Using each extended description, you would begin to improvise the scene with the pupils. A continuous process of
- improvisation • reviewing • polishing
- re-shaping • redrafting • rewriting
would occur until you and the pupils were happy with the final outcome.
Try using video to record each scene. Playback can help to develop, extend and improve the quality of the work.

(i) Scene by scene, with extra scenes to extend the story.
    Scene 1 : Emily's bedroom
    Scene 2 : At breakfast
    Scene 3 : Greenpeace respond
    Scene 4 : At school
    Scene 5 : Emily's bedroom
              Greenpeace respond
    Scene 6 : At the market
    Scene 7 : At home
    Scene 8 : Neighbours
    Scene 9 : Greenpeace respond
    Scene 10 : The empty pond
    Scene 11 : Greenpeace respond
    Scene 12 : At the seaside

(ii) **EXTENSIONS**

Scene 1
Emily's bedroom
Emily, on her own, in her room at her writing desk writing the first letter. She reads it alone.

Scene 2
The family at breakfast
Father, mother, brother and Emily. A busy morning scene, lots of business and action – maybe someone is late, something is spilt, a blouse needs ironing, the dog's been sick etc
Emily receives a letter from Greenpeace. "Look I've had a letter, they've written back. Listen, please listen...." but the family are too busy.

Scene 3
The Greenpeace Office (see Help Points)
Greenpeace read aloud the letter or we hear the response as Emily is on stage – alone. The family can either exit or freeze. The lighting can focus on Emily, e.g. a spotlight, and on Greenpeace.

Scene 4
Emily at school
In the playground – a noisy, action scene. Emily is joined by some friends. She tells them of her letter and the whale. Her friends laugh and jeer at her – use choral effects here.

e.g. **Friends A** Emily is stupid
     Emily
     Friends B She's got a whale
     Group A Sing/say their jeering phrase
     Group B Responds
     Emily is left in the middle.

As each group jeer, they are joined by others from the playground until the scene climaxes with all pupils chasing Emily. The scene ends on the teacher's whistle.

In the classroom, the pupils are doing a science project on whales. Here, the teacher can encourage pupils to tell her/him facts about whales.
Emily ends the scene by insisting that she has got a whale in her pond.

Scene 5
Emily in her bedroom
She is writing aloud another letter requesting information on food.
Greenpeace respond.

Scene 6
At the market
Market stalls – calls with a distinctive cry e.g. "lovely apples, fresh today, nice and rosy"
or "I've got a nice bit of pork my dear"
Conduct this scene like an orchestra so each cry is repeated and builds to a crescendo. Use freeze moments, miming and gesture too. Emily is searching the market for whale food but no one can help her.

Scene 7
At home
Emily writes to Greenpeace about feeding Arthur with salt, bread and cornflakes.
In the kitchen there is no bread or salt or cornflakes to be found.
Emily is sent out to ask the neighbours.

Scene 8
Neighbours
Another action scene – neighbours busy in the yards, gardens – washing cars, mowing the lawn, playing football, walking the dog, getting the bin out, trimming the hedge. This scene can be put onto tape and replayed alongside the pupils who mime or re-create their sounds.
Emily moves from neighbour to neighbour

– the sounds die out as she makes her request.
When asked who it is for, she replies that its for her whale.
This creates a stream of gossip which is passed from neighbour to neighbour and is embroidered until Emily storms off.

Scene 9
Greenpeace
Greenpeace write to Emily about the migratory habits of whales.

Scene 10
Emily by her pond
She is writing to Greenpeace – Arthur has gone.

Scene 11
Greenpeace respond
Yet another letter. This time the tone is a bit tougher.

Scene 12
The family at the seaside
Emily and her family arrive at a busy beach.
Lots of action – swimming/paddling, sunbathing, beach games, building sandcastles, eating ice cream etc.
Emily wanders to a quiet corner of the beach and there....Arthur appears.
He has come to say thank you and goodbye.
He moves off into the sea and attracts the attention – gradually – of the people on the beach
e.g. One character shouts and points others join and focus on the same point until the whole beach has come together into one compact unit – some lying down, some standing, some kneeling but all point to Arthur and Emily.
Exit Arthur.
Emily reads aloud her last letter.
THE END

STAGING THE EVENT

Split the space into three areas:
- Emily's bedroom
- Greenpeace office
- Main acting area

Emily's bedroom and the office remain static.
The furniture could be set on small raised platforms.
These provide a focus for the main characters.
Dress each set simply, using a few props to give a flavour of the venue
e.g. Emily's bedroom –
   soft toys, a bean bag, a school bag, a desk

e.g. Greenpeace office –
   desk, swivel chair, phones, in-tray, 'Greenpeace' stickers

The main acting area has no set – the performers bring on props as necessary to set the different scenes. Keep it simple, using items which are lightweight, easy to carry and representative of each scene.

The backwall of the performance can be kept bare. It could be lit using special projections overhead projector or with stage lighting effects called *gobbos* (see page 39)

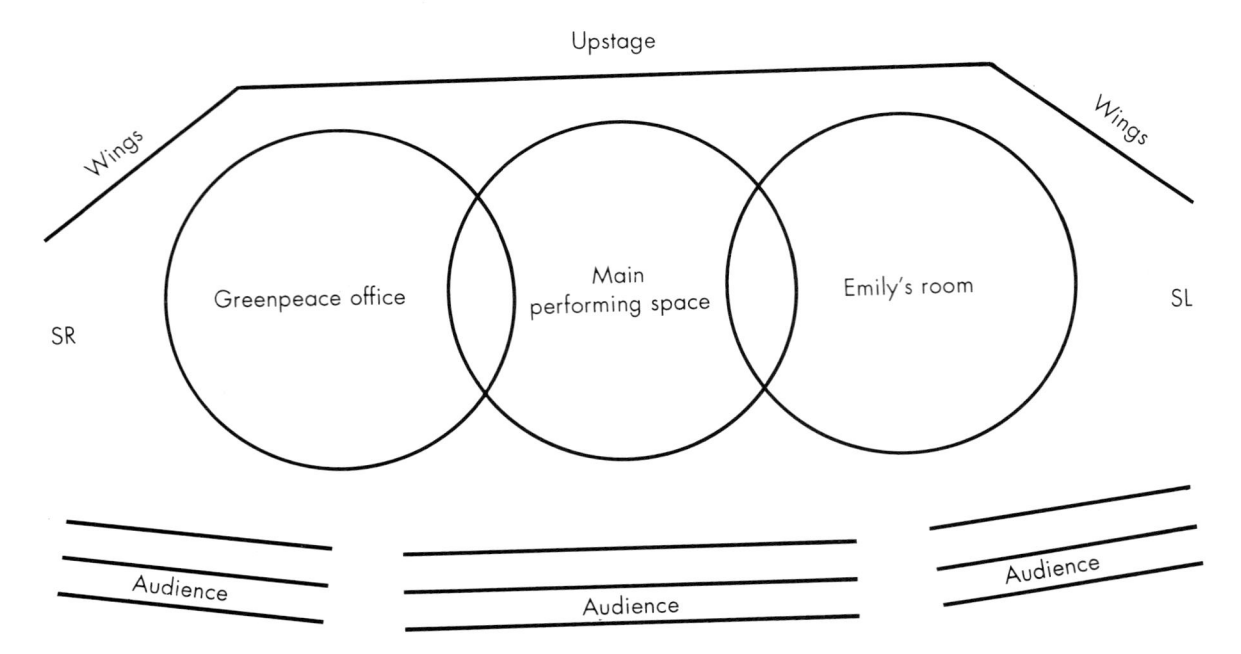

STAGE LIGHTING

Checklist

- Stage lanterns
- Resources
- Cost
- Audience
- Access
- Safety

Stage lighting has four main functions.
(1) It helps the audience see the action. It also picks out and emphasises facial expression, movement and gestures.
(2) It gives the audience a focus – it shows them where to look.
(3) It can create a special atmosphere.
(4) It marks out the performing space.

So, lighting your play can make it more effective, atmospheric and helps the performers.

Be sure that there is a good blackout. Light from windows, doors or other sources can ruin your efforts. But, if your blackout is still not 100 per cent, don't give up – continue to use lighting as this will give a different effect to ordinary room lights.

Remember – keep it simple. You do not need a vast array of complex lanterns hanging from a lighting bar. Too many lights can produce a messy, muddled effect. A simple primary lighting kit consisting of a T-bar shape which plugs into a 13 amp plug is just as effective and it is also very flexible. You hang 2 or 4 lanterns on the T-bar, extend it to its full height using the extending pole and you are now able to cover a large area with light. Add coloured gels to change moods, add 'barndoors' to stop the light flooding into unwanted spaces and get a pupil to operate the simple control and you have your play lit – all be it simply.

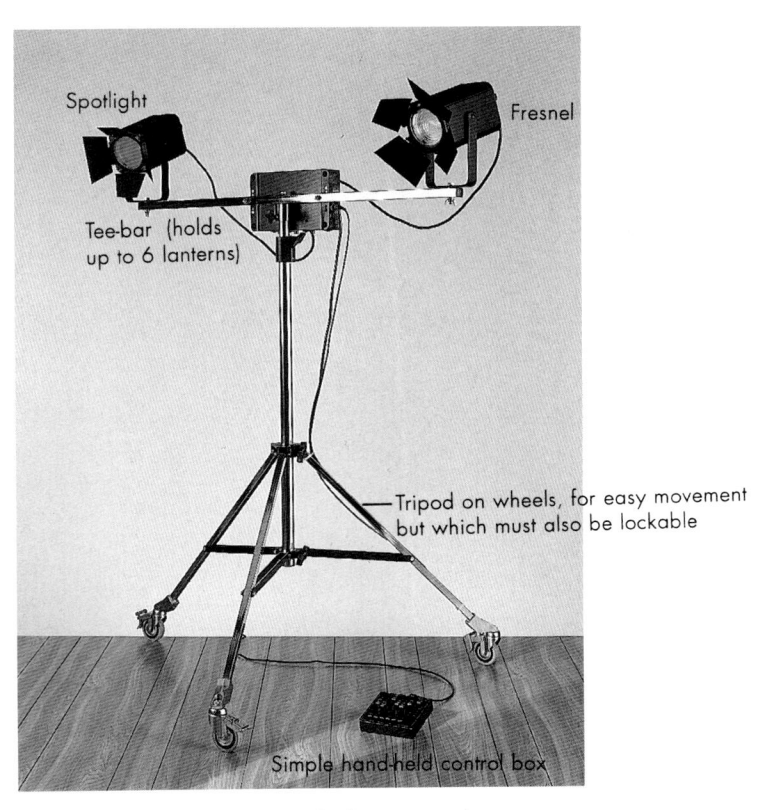

A basic primary lighting pack

STAGE LANTERNS
Four types of lantern are described here. There are many more to choose from.

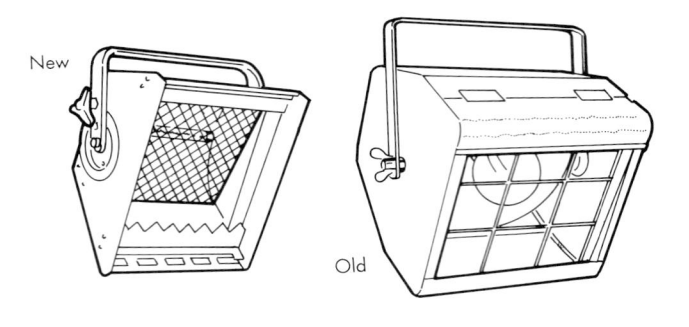

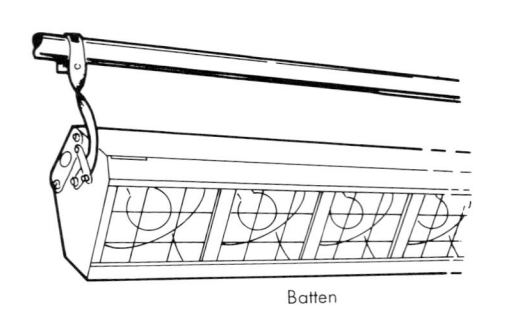

A FLOOD LIGHT
Cheap, easy to use.
They cover a lot of space but give a weak, wide beam.

You would use a floodlight to flood an area of light.

You would need several to cover a stage area.

You can add coloured gels to give some colour.

Useful for big areas.

Several floods linked together into one unit is called a *batten* (see left) and you sometimes find this hung at the back of a stage to light the back wall.

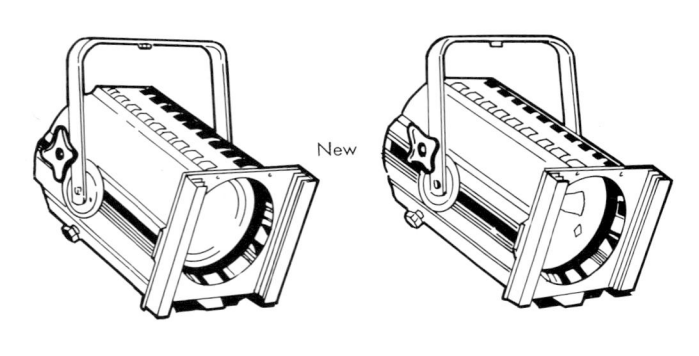

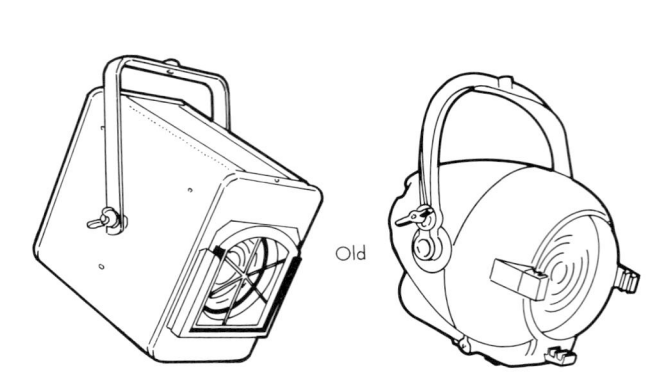

Floodlights

A FRESNEL LANTERN
This is a very useful stage lantern.
It is versatile. The light beam has a soft edge.

It can cover a wide area or can be focused down to one particular area.

Widely used. You can add coloured gels.

You can add barndoors or flaps to alter the edge of the beam in case it spills into the audience or another stage area.

These lanterns are useful on a T-bar arrangement.

Useful for lighting main action areas e.g. on the beach.

Fresnels

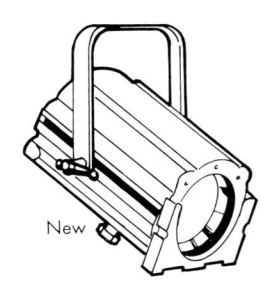

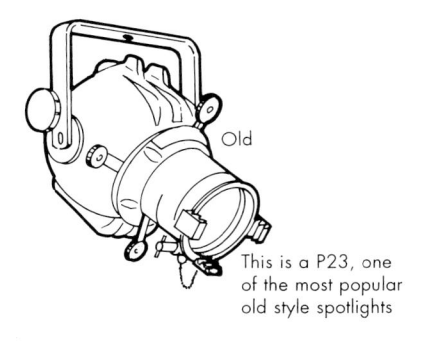

A PROFILE SPOT

This lantern gives a precise beam.

It is used to light or highlight a particular area e.g. Emily in her bedroom.

It is very useful for focusing one specific area.

You can add gobbos (which are thin tin plates cut in a pattern such as a window or tree) to give a special effect.

The spot can be hard or soft edged.

A hard edged beam is formed by using the built in shutters which are operated by small knobs found on the lantern.

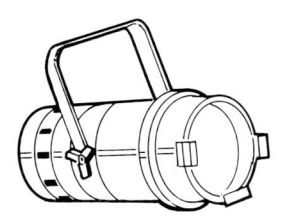

New

Old

This is a P23, one of the most popular old style spotlights

Spotlights

A PARCAN

This is a very powerful and expensive lantern.

Parcans are cheap to buy but the light bulb is very expensive.

They produce a very intense, straight beam of light which gives a brilliant special effect.

They can be used to light straight down – a long brilliant shaft of light or from side to side (useful in dance).

The intense beam is very effective with deep colours.

Great fun to use, but pricey.

A Parcan lantern

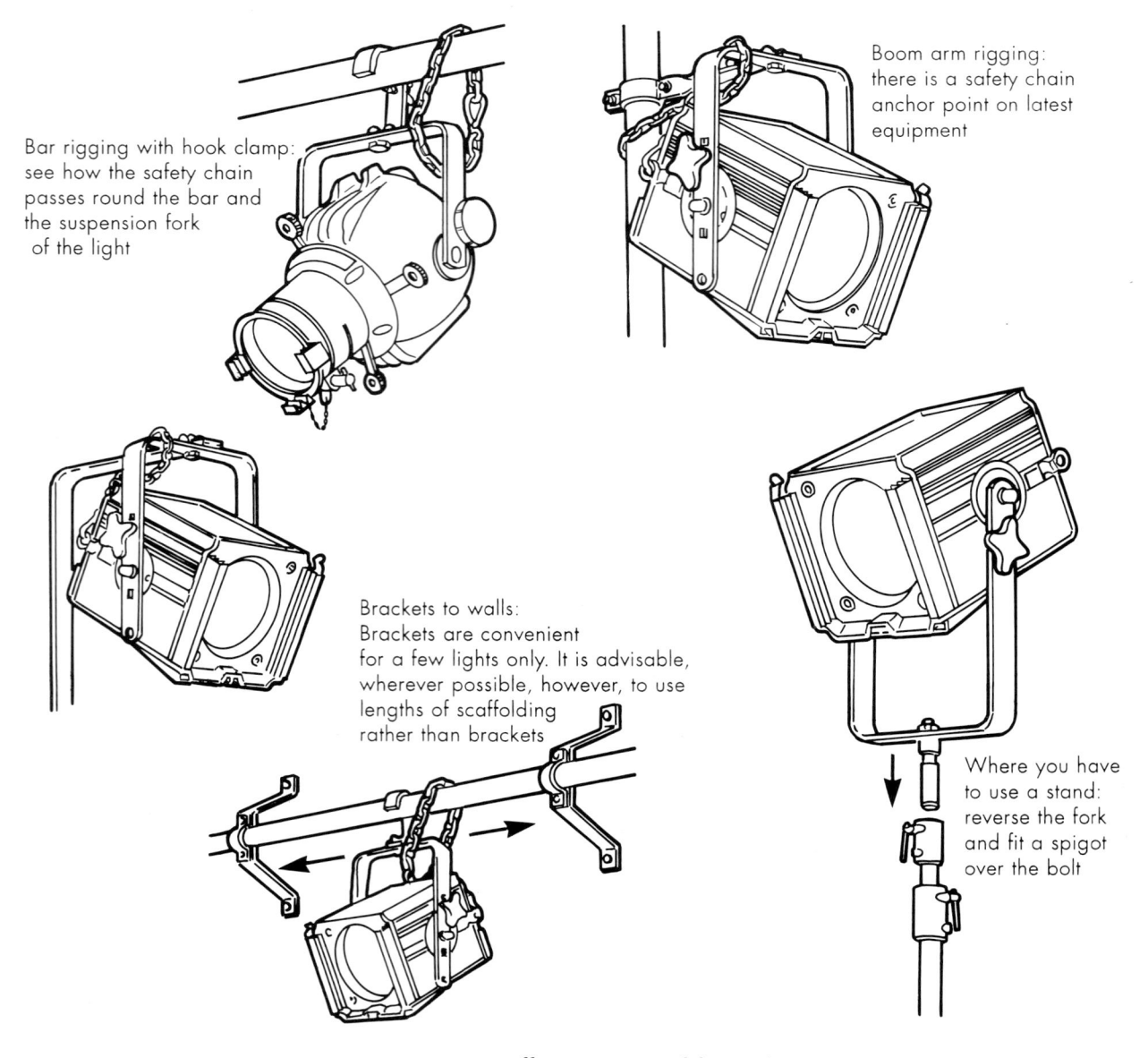

Bar rigging with hook clamp: see how the safety chain passes round the bar and the suspension fork of the light

Boom arm rigging: there is a safety chain anchor point on latest equipment

Brackets to walls: Brackets are convenient for a few lights only. It is advisable, wherever possible, however, to use lengths of scaffolding rather than brackets

Where you have to use a stand: reverse the fork and fit a spigot over the bolt

Different ways of fixing lanterns

● *Resources*

A number of outlets can help with choosing and using your lights.
- The local stage lighting suppliers. They may send a representative to give advice and show you the latest equipment. They may offer a discount to a school.
- The local secondary school, FE or HE college –
  Stage lighting is an examinable subject at GCSE, 'A' level, BTEC and degree level. With some careful planning, you could use students who may plan and rig your lights as part of their exam course. (It is a good opportunity to develop a profitable liaison!)
- Local theatre, arts centre, amateur drama group may also be able to help.

- **CARE:** be safety conscious at all times.

● *Cost*

Hiring stage lights from a supplier can be expensive.
- Try to borrow from local sources.
  If you do hire, check your needs carefully. Check the power supply you will be using so you do not overload the circuit. The school caretaker will help here or contact your local authority electrician.
- Beware of hidden costs such as extra cable, barndoors, gel frames and gobbo holders.
- If you are using gel, don't skimp. Get the correct gel for the lanterns. Cheap imitations will burn.
  Borrow from a local source such as the nearest professional theatre. They may have offcuts for you to use.
- Keep it simple – it will be cheaper.
- Plan ahead.
- Keep it safe.

Audience

Make sure that the audience can see the action! Try it out by sitting in different places in the auditorium and checking if you can see the actors.

Access

The performers need to get on and off the stage easily and safely.

Do not leave them to scrabble around in complete blackout. Blackout the scene for a few seconds to signal the end of the action then give the performers a low light or "dimout" to move in.

Torches backstage are useful in the hands of your stage management team to guide the performers.

Use luminous tape for danger spots such as steps; banisters; door jams and door handles. A little piece is adequate as it can be expensive.

Sound

Live

Use the performers to create sounds as part of the action e.g. in the neighbours' scene using only voices.

Have pupils creating sound effects as the action happens. They can be backstage and out of sight – which may mean that their sounds need amplifying through a microphone.

They can also be on stage and part of the action. It depends on your needs. It also needs good timing; clear scripting and spot-on cueing!

Here are some ways of creating live sound effects.

Rain	Take 15 to 20 dried peas and let them roll back and forth over a fine meshed wire sieve immediately beneath the microphone.
Wind	Pull a piece of silk cross two or three soft wooden boards, the strength of the wind can be adjusted by increasing or decreasing the drag.
Thunder	Either shake a large but thin piece of metal quite close to the microphone or record chords struck on a piano and play back at halfspeed.
Waves	Agitate the surface of the water in a plastic bucket and then record the sound of the water lapping against the sides.
Fire	Either crush a matchbox about two inches away from the microphone or crush a sheet of Cellophane.
Fog horn	Blow across the neck of a bottle half filled with water, the less water the bottle contains the deeper the sound.
Train	Take two wooden blocks covered with sandpaper and rub them against each other.
Horse's hoofs	Take two halves of a coconut shell and strike them together.
Footsteps in snow	Crush a small bag of flour rhythmically in front of the microphone.
Gun shot	Strike the table close to the microphone with a ruler.
Voice on telephone	Speak into a plastic or small earthenware cup close to the microphone.
Skis	Pull a small piece of wood across a rug or thick blanket at varying distances from the microphone.
Rowing boat	Dip two pieces of wood in and out of a bucket of water.
Car doors	The sound of a car door shutting can be impersonated by briskly closing the oven door.
Explosion	A really terrific explosion can be simulated with a piano by depressing all the low notes simultaneously with the loud pedal down.
Underwater caves	Record a tap dripping into a bowl at double the final speed required, then superimpose on this the voices of your subterranean explorers recorded at the slower speed and with the microphone hanging inside the piano with the loud pedal depressed.

Pre recorded sound

A number of sound effects can be recorded onto cassette and then cued in accordingly, or else you can buy pre-recorded tapes, records or CDs from which you can choose the most appropriate sounds to record yourself.

You need a good sound system and accurate cueing to make it effective.

Always check sound for levels and accuracy.

Always make 2 tapes just in case gremlins get to work on the tape system.

Music – a choice suitable to the show is a pleasant way to welcome the audience and create an atmosphere.

Music can also be useful for scene changeovers whilst a new set is being positioned.

Always check the quality of recordings and the length of the piece you are using so it is enough to cover your needs. Nothing is worse than running out of tape halfway through a scene change!

COSTUME

A BEACH BUM
black basics
add towel and sunglasses
or dayglo shorts!

EMILY
hat and T shirt with a large
'E' on the front

A SCHOOL FRIEND
basic black top and leggings
with a blazer or school
sweatshirt over the top

A MARKET TRADER
same base—
add a cap and scarf

A NEIGHBOUR
same base costume
with a cook's apron

As ever, KEEP IT SIMPLE.

The performers in the main action scenes need to have a basic costume e.g. black top and leggings so that they can add symbolic bits of costumes to represent their different roles

e.g. a school blazer or sweatshirt for school
    a kitchen apron for neighbours (man or woman)
    cap and scarf for market workers
    sunglasses and beach towel

Emily is a major role and it might be necessary to share the part between several girls.

Use one constant piece of costume to depict the role.

e.g. a baseball cap with 'E' on the front
    a T-shirt with 'E' on the front
    a netball style bib with 'E' on.

Arthur the whale, needs to make an appearance only at the end of the play in the seaside sequence.

He can be easily made using lightweight card.

Whatever materials are used – make sure it can be carried easily.

Two or three pupils could carry the whale on and operate the different flaps. They need to be dressed in long sleeved tops and leggings in black or dark blue.

Only their legs should be visible to the audience.

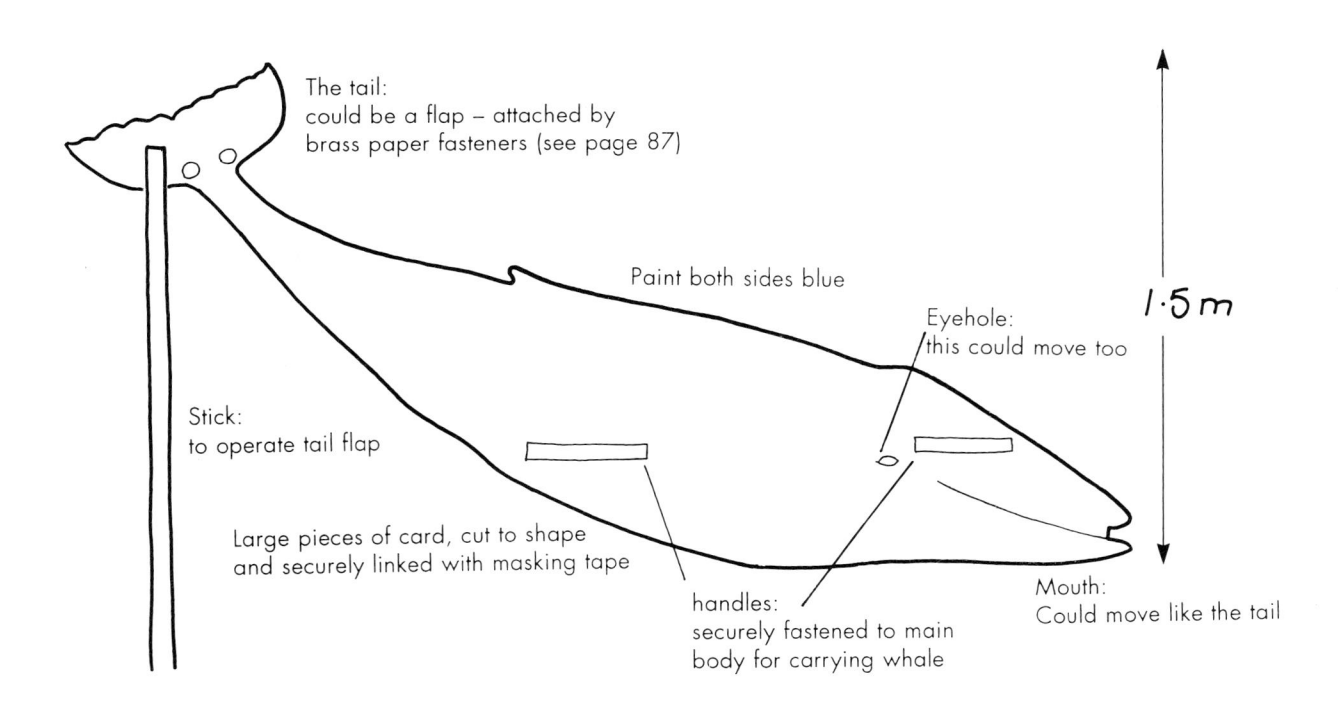

⟵——— 3 m ———⟶

The tail: could be a flap – attached by brass paper fasteners (see page 87)

Paint both sides blue

Eyehole: this could move too

1·5 m

Stick: to operate tail flap

Large pieces of card, cut to shape and securely linked with masking tape

handles: securely fastened to main body for carrying whale

Mouth: Could move like the tail

Arthur – back view

RESOURCES

Dear Greenpeace Simon James, published by Walker Books
ISBN 0 7445 1536 X

GREENPEACE
30-31 Islington Green
London
N1 8XE

- *Stage Lighting* Richard Pilbrow ISBN 1 8545 9144 4
- *Stage Lighting* Francis Reid ISBN 0 7136 3439 1
- *ABC of Stage Lighting* Francis Reid ISBN 0 7136 3609 2
- *The Staging Handbook* Francis Reid ISBN 0 7136 3289 5
- *Stage Crafts* C. Hoggett ISBN 0 7136 1557 5
- *Sound for Theatre* Graham Walne ISBN 0 8783 0119 4
- *Create Your Own Stage Sets* Terry Thomas ISBN 0 7136 3038 8
- *Safety in Live Performance* George Thompson ISBN 0 2405 1319 3
- *A Guide to Theatre Lanterns* Mark Morely, AJS Lighting Supplies,
  Hightown Industrial Estate
  Crow Lane,
  Ringwood,
  Hampshire
  01425 470888 (freephone).

  AJS provide a free Schools Advisory Service. They are also happy to supply equipment on a sale or hire basis throughout the UK.

SOUND EFFECTS: Records, tapes CDs
BBC Enterprises
Woodlands
80 Wood Lane
London
W2 0TT
0181 576 2216

THE GREAT EXHIBITION PROJECT

Crystal Palace, 1851, where the Great Exhibition was held

INTRODUCTION

The Great Exhibition Project can become part of the historical core study unit on Victorian Britain. It is a way of combining performance and class-based study. It is also a clear focus for a wide ranging and popular study unit.

The aims of this performance project are to:
develop the skills of physical imaging initiated with the 'Instant Assembly Model';
develop characterisation;
study and create costumes and props appropriate to the characters, linking all aspects with a story set in **The Great Exhibition of 1851.**

The way into the project is through a range of drama activities which teach specific skills including physical imaging and encourage the development of improvisation skills.

Running alongside this skills-based work would be the class-based topic exploring Victorian Britain. This can be a vast and intimidating topic. This project gives you one route into the historical period which, whilst focussing on one event, accesses pupils to a range of facts, evidence and information. In particular, it can provide a purpose for research into scientific and industrial achievement; the structure and layers of Victorian Society; design; The Empire; lives of ordinary people; music; art and drama of the period.

It is a simple idea based on the Crystal Palace building which housed the Great Exhibition of 1851.

The pupils play 2 main roles – a character(s) and part of the exhibition building!

The characters are all linked by their visit to the exhibition.

Recreating the Crystal Palace is daunting so use the pupils and their bodies in a simple but effective use of imaging. It is then, imaginative, fun and informative. As it's drama, anything is possible, including sections of the building speaking facts or thoughts aloud! At the same time, the characters come to life and, through short cameos, give a story about their lives and their journey to the exhibition.

A narrator in role as a news reporter provides the links, plus music and songs of the period help to create the atmosphere. The audience could even have a song sheet to join in!

Finally, Queen Victoria arrives to open the exhibition as the performance piece reaches its climax.

Ideas for curricular extensions are given in *Curricular Links* alongside aspects of drama which can be taught through this project, in the *Dramatic Curriculum*.

Fact File about the exhibition could provide your speaking building with its script.

In *Creating the Story* the simple story is set, characters introduced, and a running order is suggested. As ever, the running order is extended to give the characters a fuller content to develop through improvising in class.

The *Production Techniques* section gives ideas for simple and inexpensive costumes; staging ideas and props (pages 57).

Once again the theme is simplicity, with the focus on the characters and the Crystal Palace.

Every project needs organising but this one has a regular pattern of narrator – character story – narrator etc until the climax with the arrival of Victoria. There is plenty of opportunity for a number of pupils to be involved if you want to make it a year group event or you could keep numbers quite low by just using a handful of pupils to play a number of characters. Simple costume changes can help this approach.

Try it and see how Victorian Britain can come to life in a simple but different way!

The Great Exhibition project is a good framework for study because:

"We can dress up as Victorian children and pretend to go to school in those times"

"My granny has got a flat iron – given to her by her granny"

"The headteacher has got a cane locked away in his cupboard!"

"We can ride on a steam train"

"Lots to do"

"There is lots of resource material available"

"We can visit the living museum"

"We can get hold of the census for the period"

"The hospital used to be a workhouse"

"The influence of the Victorians is still felt today"

"Its within living memory"

"We've got a family bible that goes that far back"

"We've still got the costumes from Oliver"

"I can use Dickens as a class reader"

"Our school building is 150 years old"

CURRICULAR LINKS

SCIENCE
- Inventions e.g. the telephone; steam engines; photography
- Medical developments – anaesthetics/antiseptics
- Personalities – Lister, Pasteur, Nightingale
- Public health and disease
- Nutrition

HISTORY
- The Empire
- Trade
- Industrial revolution
- Social reform
- Housing
- Child labour
- Education
- Life at home
- Rich and poor
- Family trees

TECHNOLOGY
- Artefacts
- Machines
- Steam power
- Inventions

ART
- Artists and craftworkers
- Architecture and buildings
- Printing
- Textile developments
- Sculpture

R.E.
- The range of worship and religions
- The Salvation Army
- The spread of Christianity through missionaries

GEOGRAPHY
- The canal system
- The railway
- Migration
- The world map
- Explorers
- Local studies
- Growth of towns

DANCE/PE
- Historical review
- Sport and leisure
- Games

DRAMA
- Melodrama
- Victorian music hall traditions
- In role days e.g. Victorian school
- At the court of Queen Victoria – role play

MUSIC
- Songs
- Instruments
- Composers

MATHS
- Census
- Trade figures
- Time lines
- Money

LANGUAGE
- Letters
- Newspapers
- Famous writers
- Advertising

THE DRAMATIC CURRICULUM

This project provides ample opportunity to cover some aspects of the drama curriculum.

	Key Stage 1	Key Stage 2
MAKING	Pretending to be someone from a long time ago. Telling a story through drama. Making up a play. Playing a part.	Developing new drama conventions. e.g. physical theatre. Creating role using appropriate styles of language. Developing work from improvisation.
PERFORMING	Sharing a play with others. Using a costume. Singing and dancing.	Performing to an audience as part of an ensemble. Acting out different roles. Using costume and props.
RESPONDING	Telling a friend what it was like to be in a play as a different person.	Understanding how their play reflects the historical period. Developing ideas to improve the devising and performance process.

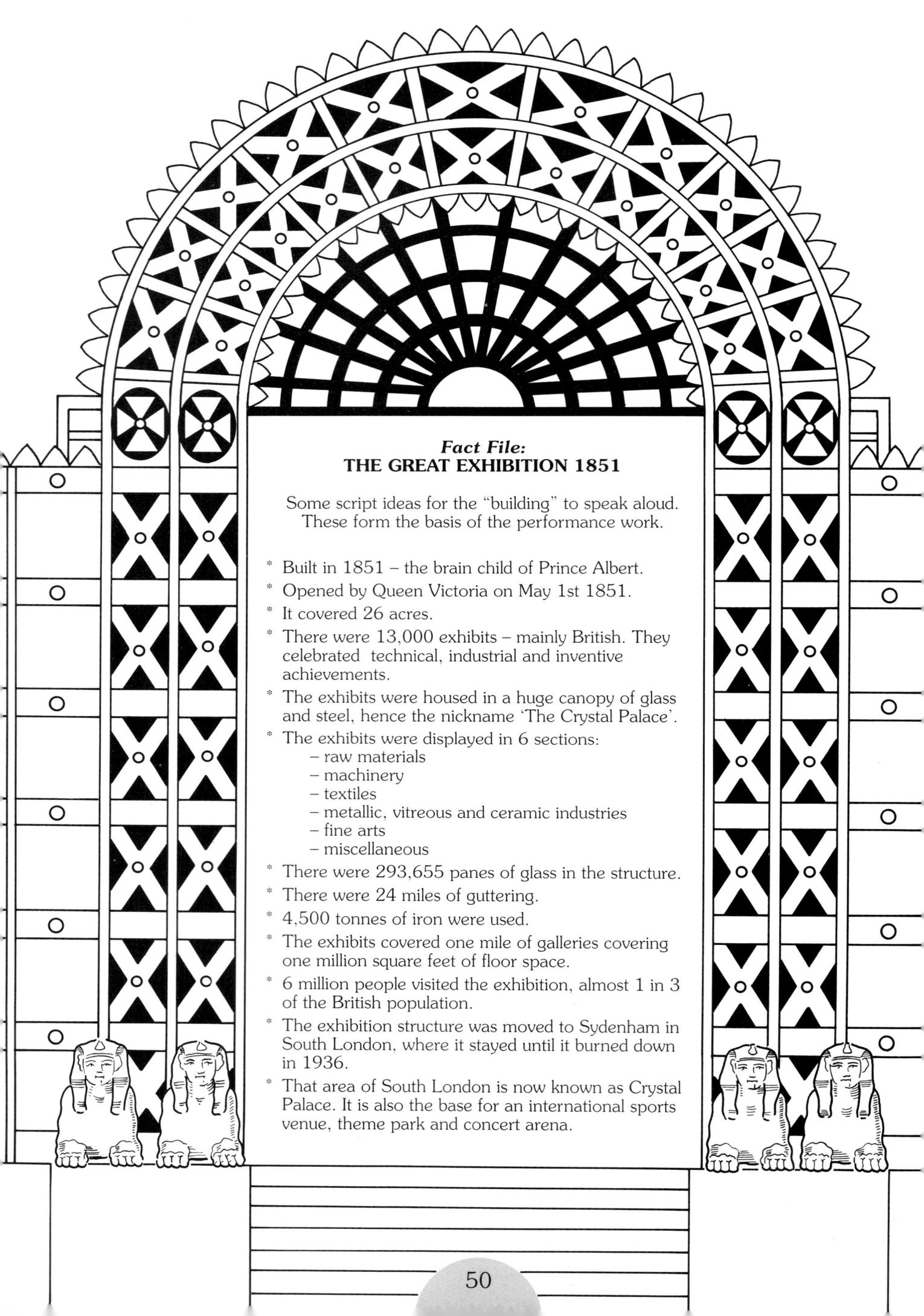

Fact File:
THE GREAT EXHIBITION 1851

Some script ideas for the "building" to speak aloud.
These form the basis of the performance work.

* Built in 1851 – the brain child of Prince Albert.
* Opened by Queen Victoria on May 1st 1851.
* It covered 26 acres.
* There were 13,000 exhibits – mainly British. They celebrated technical, industrial and inventive achievements.
* The exhibits were housed in a huge canopy of glass and steel, hence the nickname 'The Crystal Palace'.
* The exhibits were displayed in 6 sections:
    – raw materials
    – machinery
    – textiles
    – metallic, vitreous and ceramic industries
    – fine arts
    – miscellaneous
* There were 293,655 panes of glass in the structure.
* There were 24 miles of guttering.
* 4,500 tonnes of iron were used.
* The exhibits covered one mile of galleries covering one million square feet of floor space.
* 6 million people visited the exhibition, almost 1 in 3 of the British population.
* The exhibition structure was moved to Sydenham in South London, where it stayed until it burned down in 1936.
* That area of South London is now known as Crystal Palace. It is also the base for an international sports venue, theme park and concert arena.

CREATING THE STORY

Finding the focus

Where do you start?

The project described in this chapter was stimulated by an old photograph of the Crystal Palace in Hyde Park.

Victorian drama project = The Great Exhibition of 1851

Curriculum focus – Victorian scientific and
 – industrial achievement
 – social class structure
 – architecture and design
 – the Empire.

With such a wide and rich topic, many other projects could also be initiated. Try and focus in on one area, this could arise from:

your personal research
e.g. the local F.E. college was once a workhouse.

Victorian drama project = life in the workhouse.

Curriculum focus = social reform
 The life of poor people during Victorian times.

A pupil's research
e.g. one of the pupils brings in an old photo of the school taken in 1860.

Victorian drama project = a Victorian school day.

Curriculum focus – the life of a school child
 – moral and social welfare
 – the Victorian curriculum.

A parent's artefact
e.g. they donate a Gladstone bag belonging to their family to the class display.

Victorian drama project = upstairs and downstairs or life as a parlourmaid in the house of a rich factory owner.

Curriculum focus – Industrial Revolution
 – the class structure
 – social reform

The story outline

The project is based on events that occurred on 1st May 1851 in Hyde Park, London.

Queen Victoria is about to open the Crystal Palace built from an idea by her beloved Albert.

Thousands of British and European inventions; business magnets exhibitors and designers use the opportunity to display their extensive scientific and industrial achievements.

The crowds attending the exhibition are drawn from all walks of life. Some are rich, some are poor but they all have a story to tell.

This project celebrates not only scientific achievements but the individuals who created Victorian society.

The Characters

Queen Victoria
Albert
The royal household

An exhibitor and his family

A Duke and his family

A doctor and his family

A farmer and his family

A factory worker and her family

A factory owner and his family

A maid and her soldier beau

A news reporter (the narrator)

How to Start

(1) Begin by choosing parts.
(2) Using research documents, books, church registers, local census material even a Dickens novel, encourage pupils to choose names and to **devise a short character outline.**

MY CHARACTER FACT SHEET.

MY NAME IS .... OLD
I AM ....
I LIVE AT ....
I LIVE WITH ....
MY JOB IS ....
I LIKE ....
I DISLIKE ....
MY HOPES FOR THE FUTURE ARE ....
....
MY FEARS FOR THE FUTURE ARE ....
....
I WANT TO GO TO THE EXHIBITION BECAUSE ....

HERE IS A PICTURE OF ME:

They can do this as a solo activity or as a family unit.

(3) Each group then forms **a family portrait** for the local photographer using the still image strategy (see page 9).
Use a traditional Victorian photograph to give pupils the shape of the pose.
They all freeze.
Then one character comes to life, steps out of the picture and introduces their family giving a brief pen portrait on their character fact sheet.
This can also be written down to formulate a script.
These short scenes can be included in the presentation.

Then draw the family portrait for display material as a visual reminder for later work.

(4) Run several group photos together to get a flavour of different families. Keep spoken parts short and precise.

(5) **HOTSEATING:** Use this strategy in class. One pupil takes on a role in the play and sits in "the hot seat". The rest of the class, out of role, ask prepared questions to this pupil. It gives the pupils an opportunity to establish detail of their roles. This will help pupils to fix their characters firmly in their heads and can also help to develop more facts about the characters in your play. Some questions you could ask are: 'Why are you going to the exhibition?' 'Can you afford to take all your family to the exhibition?' 'How will you travel to London?'

PHYSICAL IMAGING

This drama strategy is an extension of the still image (see Cinderella section). In teaching pupils to use this idea you have access to a complete set of props including the Crystal Palace itself!

So teach the technique :

(1) Sculptors and statues : get pupils into pairs.
(2) Decide who is A and B.
(3) A is to be the statue. He/she is a large piece of modelling clay.
(4) B is the sculptor who is to gently mould his/her partner into a secret shape.
(5) As teacher, you devise cards onto which you write the object that the sculptor is to make. Only the sculptors see this!
(6) A has to guess the shape that B has moulded him/her into.
(7) Practise with human shapes first e.g. a dancer, a mechanic, a nurse or Queen Victoria!
(8) Then introduce inanimate objects which relate to the performance piece e.g. a stone lion, a large pot plant, a fountain.
(9) Swap roles so everyone tries sculpting and moulding.
(10) Remember to always relate games or exercises to the topic. This gives them a purpose and learning intention.

Having used this drama exercise, show them some pictures of exhibits from the Great Exhibition e.g. a fountain, a steam engine, a gas lamp, Queen Victoria's carriage (see resources section, page 60).

Using the same technique, get them to mould themselves as a group of 6 into these shapes.
Share.
Add and extend.
Bring to life using sound and movement.

Now for the Crystal Palace.
Focus the pupils onto this task by referring them to several TV and magazine adverts for building societies and banks where houses, wedding cakes and bridges are portrayed by a large group of people forming the shape of these objects.
Now show them a picture of the Crystal Palace : An OHT projected onto a blank wall gives a good impression of size.
Ask them to point out the main features of the building e.g. the main arch steps, stone lions.

Carefully, two by two, create the central archway, in the style of the old 'Oranges and Lemons' game
e.g.

Main Arch

Add side arches, lions statues and at the end of the central arch add the fountain previously created by a group, to form a focus.

Using the facts on the resources page – give each arch and feature one fact to learn.

The Crystal Palace can come to life in speech and form using only pupil power!

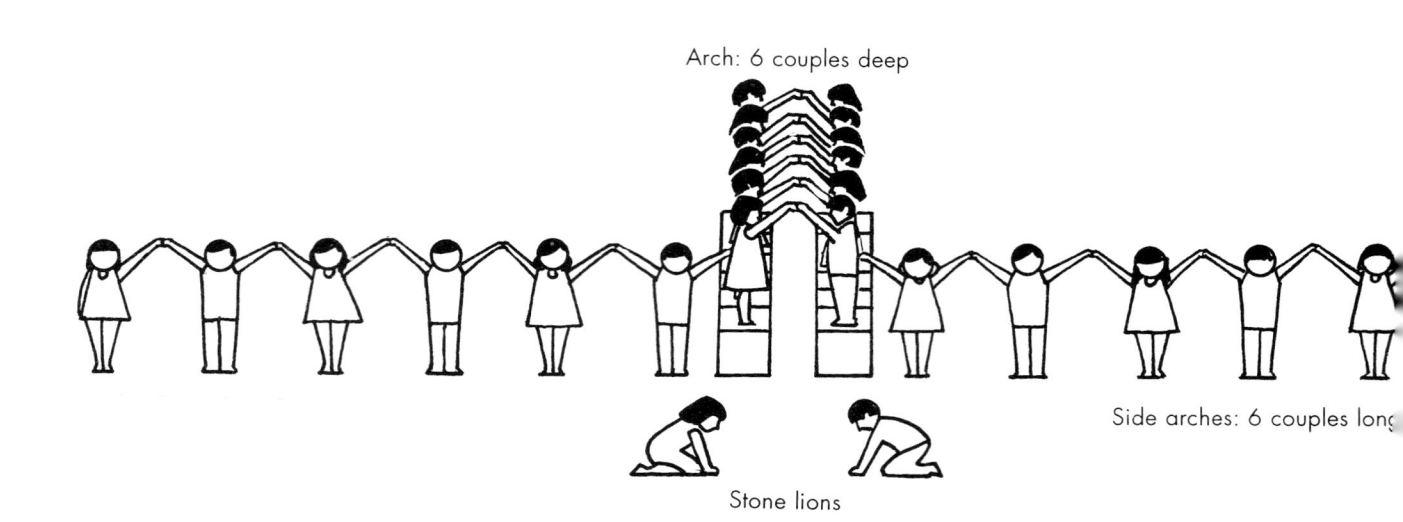

Arch: 6 couples deep

Side arches: 6 couples long

Stone lions

SUGGESTIONS FOR A RUNNING ORDER

(this can be scripted)

Music

Narrator sets the story : the stories of 6 groups of Victorian people whose lives are linked by a trip to see the Great Exhibition of 1851.

Scene 1
Opening scene is the same as the final picture, that of all the groups finally arrived at The Great Exhibition.
Each story group comes to life at once to give a busy cameo of their life, their dilemma, and how they nearly failed to arrive.

Freeze

In turn each story is acted out as a complete story. The dilemmas and their solutions are shared with the audience e.g.

Scene 2 The Royal stories
Music/cast song – plus narrator.

Scene 3 The Exhibitor's story
Music link – plus narrator.

Scene 4 The Farmer's story
Music link – plus narrator.

Scene 5 The Factory Worker's story
Music link – plus narrator.

Scene 6 The Factory Owner's story
Music link – plus narrator.

Scene 7 The Maid's story
Music link – plus narrator.
Moment of arrival and their spoken thoughts as they see the building for the first time.

Scene 8 The Crystal Palace is built by cast.

Scene 9 The building speaks as narrator moves around it.
Narrator announces that Queen Victoria is on route.

Scene 10 Cast create Victoria's carriage (see Cinderella, page 12) complete with Queen Victoria and Albert on board, waving to the crowds as the carriage moves around the stage. Narrator leads real audience in cheers and applause for the Queen.
Queen Victoria enters the palace.
She walks amongst the cast structure and then requests to see some exhibits.
Cast reassemble into exhibits e.g. fountain, gas lamp or even crazy exhibits from the future. Narrator acts as host.
Queen Victoria speaks to some of the characters from the stories.

Scene 11 Story groups set out on their return journey, speaking thoughts aloud of their great day.

Scene 12 Groups reassemble into original pose. Narrator closes performance.
Picture projected onto 4th wall as cast exit.

Music to end.

Extending the story

So far you have got a list of characters, a place, a time, and an event. In order to catch your audience's attention you need an injection of TENSION in the form of a problem or a dilemma which befall some of your characters.
Here are some ideas:

---

1. THE ROYAL HOUSEHOLD:
THE UPSTAIRS STORY – Prince Albert is fretting over the exhibition. The costs are huge and the Government refuses any financial aid. Who will give him financial support and at what price? Why have the Government refused him help?
THE DOWNSTAIRS STORY – A maid accidentally trips over the dress Queen Victoria is to wear at the opening. It is badly torn. What does she do now? She is always in trouble but needs to keep her job to help pay for medicines for her sickly mother.

---

5. THE FACTORY OWNER'S STORY: The soap factory wins a huge order for scented soap for an ocean liner company. The soap factory is nearly saved from closure by this order. It will mean all holidays are to be cancelled and the workers are angry especially when they find out that the owner is to go to London to the Great Exhibition whilst they toil and lose their holidays.

---

2. THE EXHIBITOR'S STORY:
The original idea for a steam powered potato picker came from Marigold, the office girl. This unscrupulous exhibitor has stolen her idea and sold it as his own. He plans to take all the glory at The Great Exhibition until his wife and daughter find the original plans and confront him with the theft.

---

3. THE FARMER'S STORY:
The farmer enjoys the old ways of farming his land using traditional methods. His son wants to introduce new ideas and machinery. The two argue until the women in the family decide that a trip to see the Crystal Palace could solve matters once and for all.

---

6. THE MAID'S STORY:
Violet is to meet her soldier beau : Sgt. Dan Evans at The Great Exhibition. Her mother is against her courting a soldier and locks her in her room. What does Violet do now?

---

4. THE FACTORY WORKER'S STORY:
The trip of a lifetime is all planned. The girls have saved for months to send Molly and her new husband on a special honeymoon trip. They have been promised a day's leave for Molly until the factory owner stops all holidays and wants all workers to do overtime on the day of the planned trip. The workers have had enough of poor treatment at work but can they afford to risk their jobs in the soap factory for the sake of Molly and Bob?

THE PRODUCTION TECHNIQUES

Costumes

Keep it simple by using accessories to suggest roles. Pupils will enjoy making simple costumes and it keeps cost and fuss to a minimum.

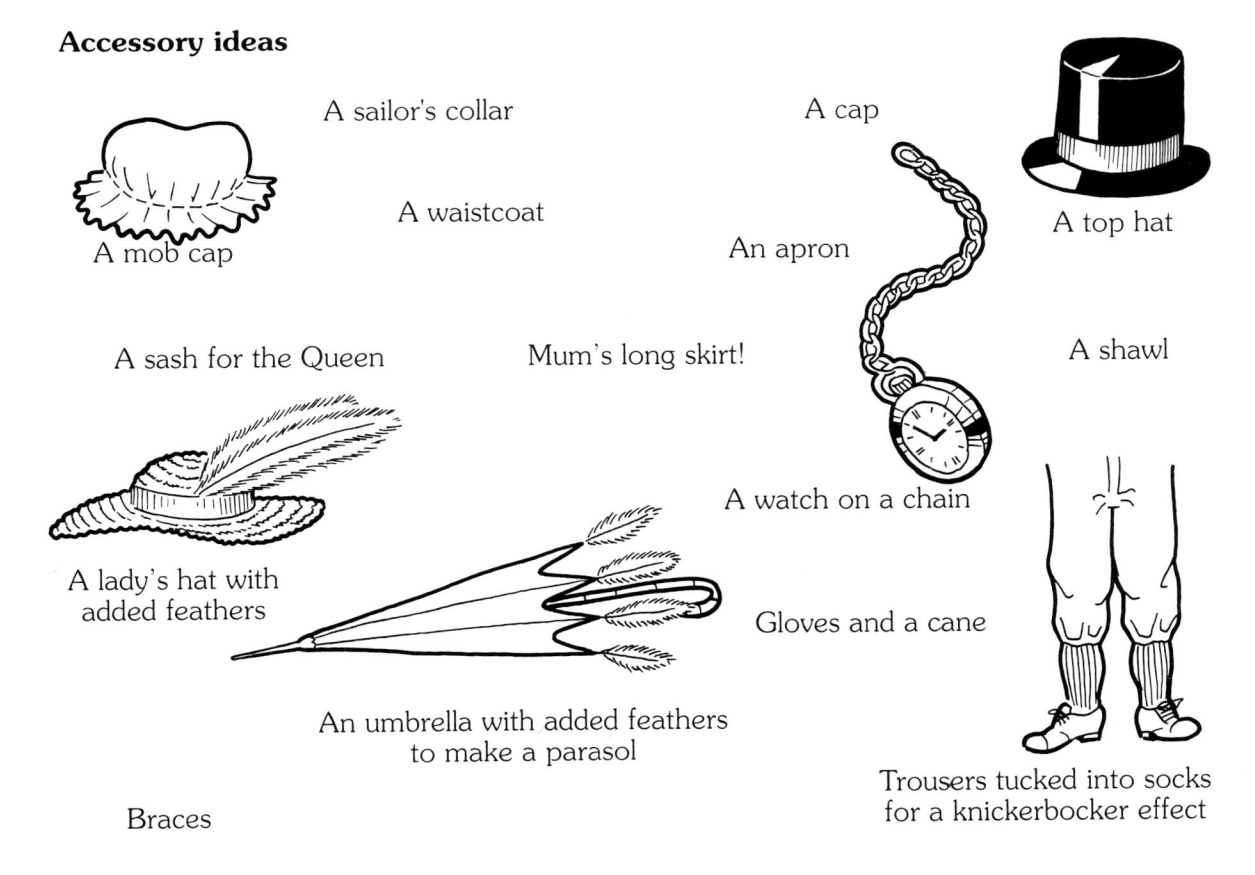

Accessory ideas

A mob cap

A sailor's collar

A waistcoat

A cap

An apron

A top hat

A sash for the Queen

Mum's long skirt!

A shawl

A lady's hat with added feathers

A watch on a chain

An umbrella with added feathers to make a parasol

Gloves and a cane

Braces

Trousers tucked into socks for a knickerbocker effect

Add these to the pupils day-to-day clothing to give a suggestion of the role they are playing. If they are playing several roles, then quick changes are kept simple.

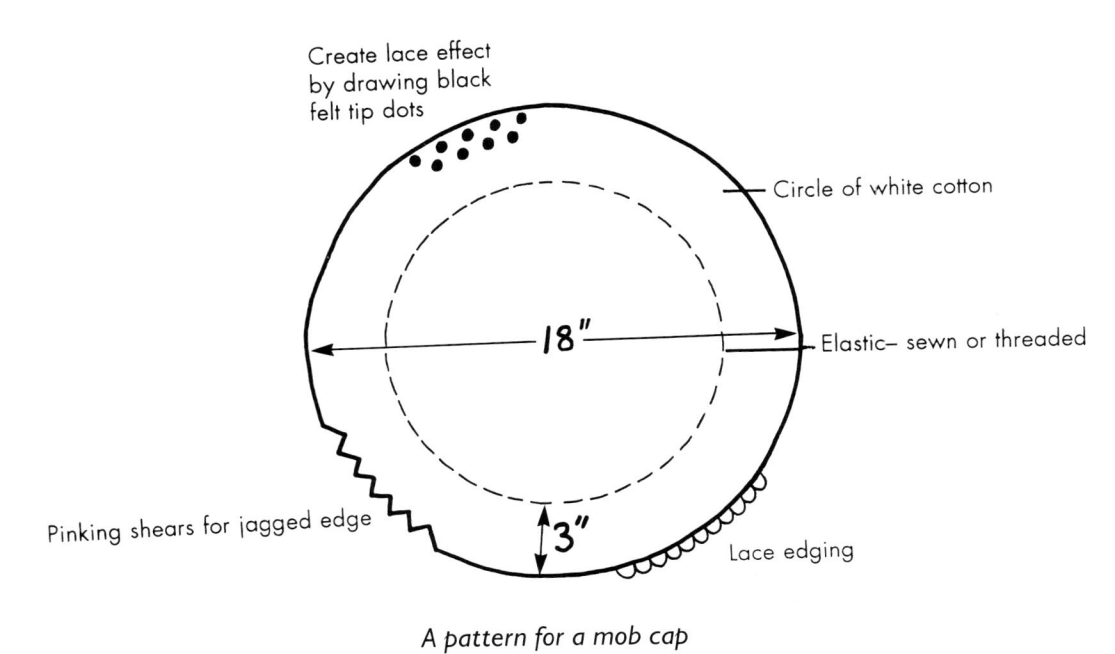

Create lace effect by drawing black felt tip dots

Circle of white cotton

18"

Elastic– sewn or threaded

Pinking shears for jagged edge

3"

Lace edging

A pattern for a mob cap

57

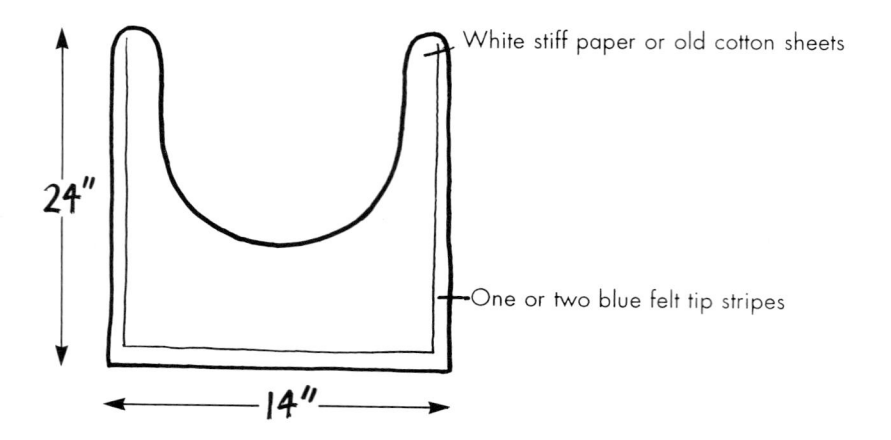

A pattern for a sailor's collar

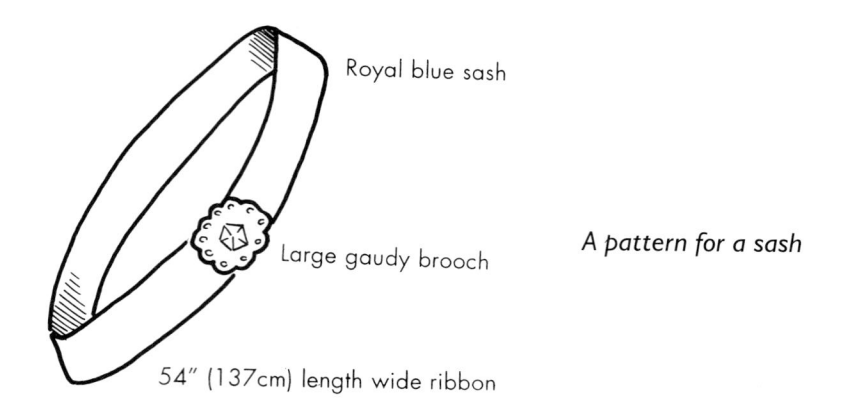

- White stiff paper or old cotton sheets
- One or two blue felt tip stripes
- 24"
- 14"

A pattern for a sash

- Royal blue sash
- Large gaudy brooch
- 54" (137cm) length wide ribbon

PROPS

Victorian items are available from attics and family heirlooms but these are delicate and old! In the hurly burly of performing they can easily be damaged.

The next section suggests a way, using Drama, to create props at no expense!

STAGING THE EVENT

(1) Seat the audience on the floor on 3 sides, as shown in the diagram.

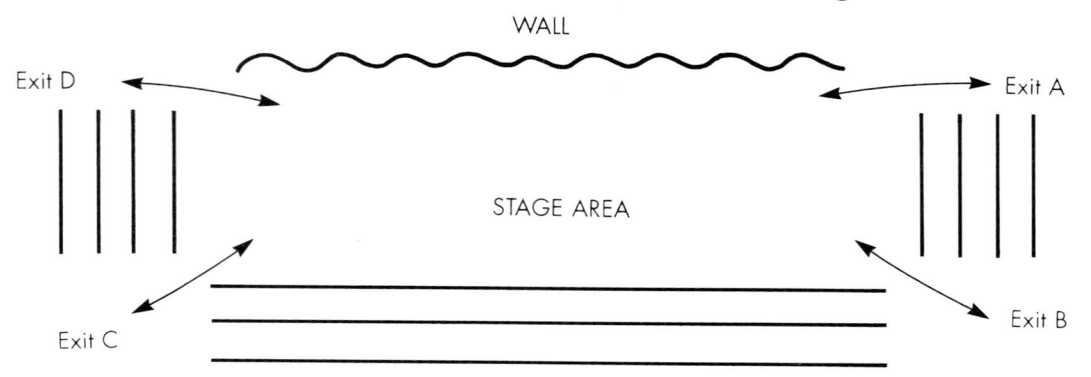

WALL

Exit D   Exit A

STAGE AREA

Exit C   Exit B

(2) Use music to set the atmosphere e.g. parlour songs, patriotic songs such as Rule Britannia.

(3) Slides projected onto the 4th wall of events in Victorian Times can be shown, accompanied by music at the start and end of the performance and as scene change fillers.

Crystal Palace

Queen Victoria and family

A steam engine

(4) Give the audience a song sheet with the words of any well known songs that you use in the play so they can join in the song as well. You could even have the narrator as the Master of Ceremonies urging the audience to join in the singing at an appropriate moment.

(5) Use a narrator to link the items together. Their role could be:
   a) A Master of Ceremonies in a music hall introducing each part of the play and adding a commentary to set the scene. They can also get the audience to join in the communal songs.
   b) A modern day school child researching their Victorian project and finding a book in their granny's attic.
   c) A Victorian news reporter writing their story.
   d) A time traveller from another planet who has landed in 1851.
   e) A Victorian child recalling the great day in her diary.

Books for the Library

Victorian Britain, History in Evidence series, Wayland ISBN 1 8521 0582 8
Good blend of illustrations of contemporary prints, objects etc. Accessible text

Victorian Children, A & C Black ISBN 0 7136 1324 6
Top juniors. Lots of contemporary illustrations, wide range of aspects of life covered. Informative text.

How We Used to Live, A & C Black ISBN 0 7136 3310 7
Excellent range of pictorial sources. Useful text.

When I was young – early 20th century, Franklin Watts ISBN 0 8631 3872 1
Example from an interesting series that looks at aspects of the life of a named individual in a most attractive and accessible way. Strictly, this book moves just outside the Victorian period, but still very usable.

Turn of the Century series from A & C Black. An excellent series, with fascinating details and many photographs of modern children with artefacts, in museum 'room' settings. (These could be used selectively in KS1 too)

Babies	0 7136 3353 0
In the Post	0 7136 3184 8
School Day	0 7136 3185 6
Breakfast	0 7136 3186 4
Washday	0 7136 3183 X
Christmas	0 7136 3350 6
Rubbish	0 7136 3351 4
Keeping Clean	0 7136 3352 2

Finding out about... series. Lots of snippets of source material. A very useful quarry. Older juniors only.

Victorian Country Life	0 7134 43510
Victorian Law and Order	0 7134 5659 0
Victorian Social Reformers	0 7134 5051 7
Victorian London	0 7134 4745 1
Women in 19th Century Britain	0 7134 5049 5
Seaside Holidays	0 7134 4439 8

THE SERPENT KING PROJECT

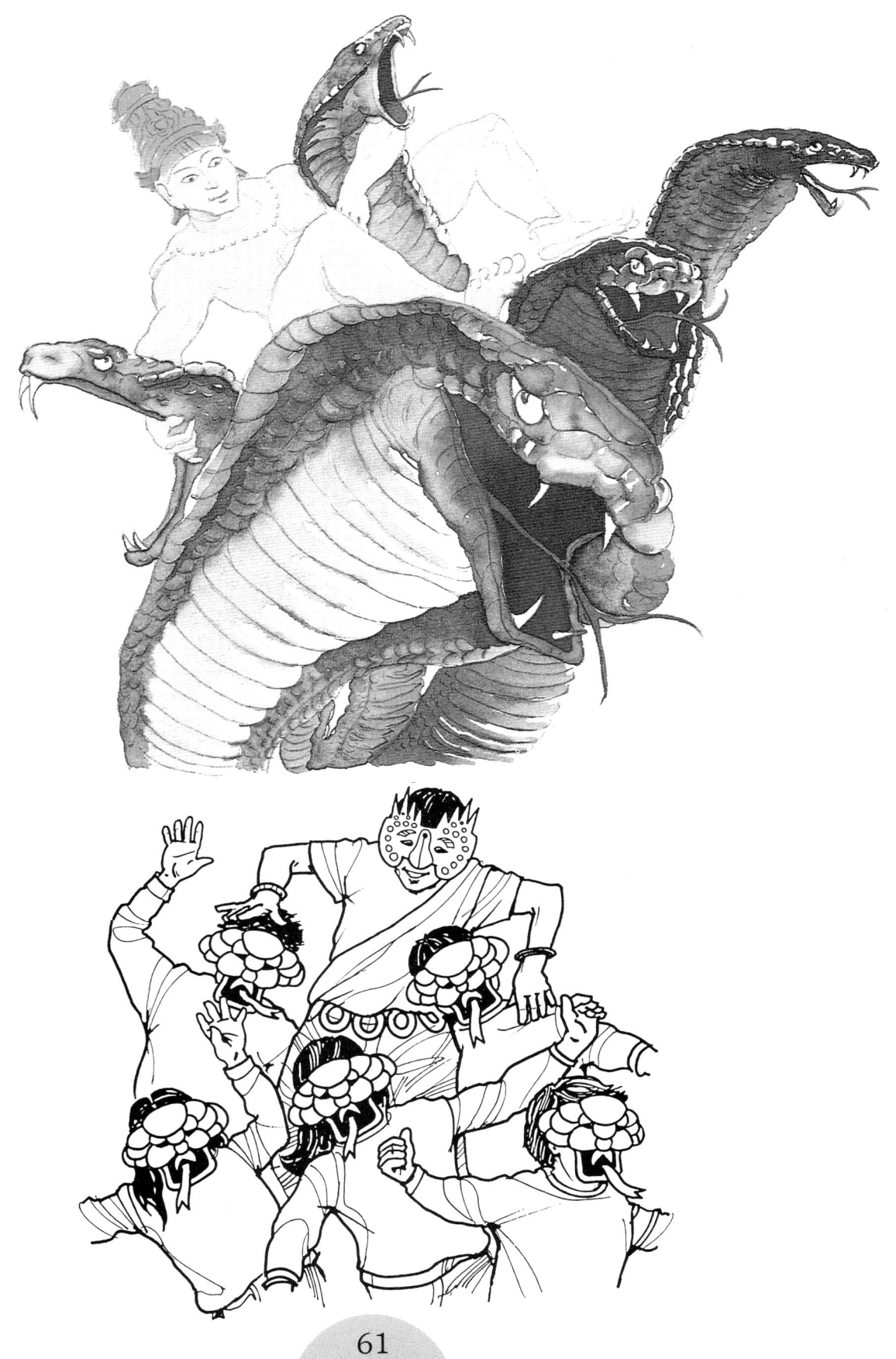

INTRODUCTION

This project will give some simple mask-making ideas and show how they can be used to enhance a performance piece based on an Asian folk tale.

Pupils love using masks – even the shy ones as they can step into the character and hide behind its mask.

Using masks encourages the development of non-verbal communication skills such as mime, movement and gesture. All these aspects of performance become larger than life and more meaningful as the mask comes to life.

Eye masks, half masks or full face masks are quick, easy and cheap to create, fun to use and can transform a play. You can buy ready-made masks such as horror faces or representations of famous people. Making your own mask and learning to communicate through it is a more meaningful and enjoyable process.

As ever, the simpler the mask, the more effective it is.

The story in the project *The Serpent King* comes from India and is a folktale from the Hindu religion. Indian culture, along with many others has a long tradition of using masks in its theatrical performances.

The same, simple approach as laid out in the 'Instant Assembly Model' is again used – the story is broken up into manageable scenes. The main characters are identified and extra ones are created to enhance the story.

The starting point is, as before, a still image. The whole story could be enacted using this basic method with each character wearing a mask and the story told by a narrator. This approach would suit younger pupils or inexperienced pupils.

Extensions or activating strategies are offered to bring each scene to life.

A narrator is a useful device to help move the story along. Each scene could be a mixture of mime, dialogue and movement. If each character is wearing a half mask the the dialogue could be heard. If a full mask is used, the dialogue could be muffled. This is where a narrator could step in as the dialogue is recorded onto tape and replayed. Special sound effects could be added to create an exciting atmosphere.

The vital point to remember is that the use of masks is dependent upon appropriate movements and gestures to bring it to life.

Work on Indian dance movements would enhance the project. It is a great opportunity to bring in a professional artist to work alongside the pupils to develop movement s and dances which are appropriate to the story.

Ideas for making masks – simply and inexpensively are given. There are many other ways to create masks and the ideas on offer here have been tried and tested in schools. Simple make-up ideas are also given along with some handy hints to help stage and costume the project.

The most fun will be had in creating a five-headed snake just using the pupils. The snake has to move and speak. It also needs to give the impression of being a very important snake which rules the underwater world. This task not only enhances the story but also demands that pupils must co-operate in their group in order to devise the creature.

The Serpent King is a good project because:

- It breaks up easily into simple scenes
- It could involve all the class
- There is a lot of action
- Each group could work on one scene
- Krishna is 12 years old: he is close in age to the class
- It fits into the topic on 'India'
- It could be performed just using frozen pictures – quick and easy
- It is a moral story of good versus evil
- It fits into the RE studies
- Lots of opportunities for dance and music
- There are lots of settings
- It could act as a springboard for research into other Asian studies
- Great for assembly
- It involves fighting – though slow motion!
- We have to create a 5-headed monster: great for technology and art

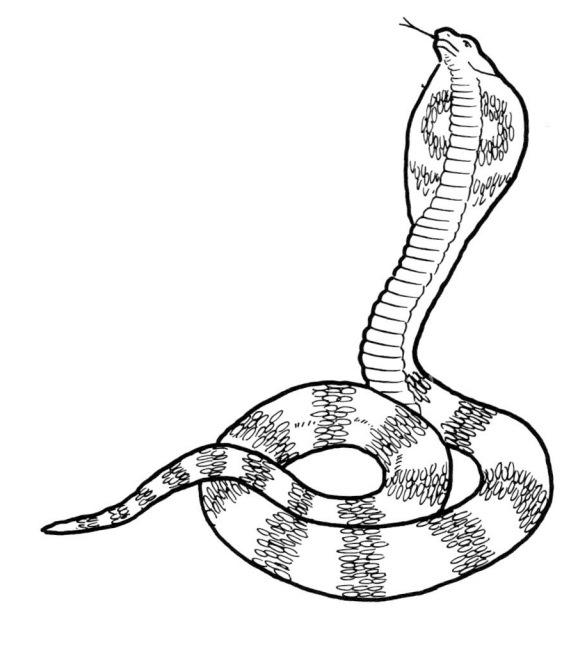

CROSS-CURRICULAR LINKS

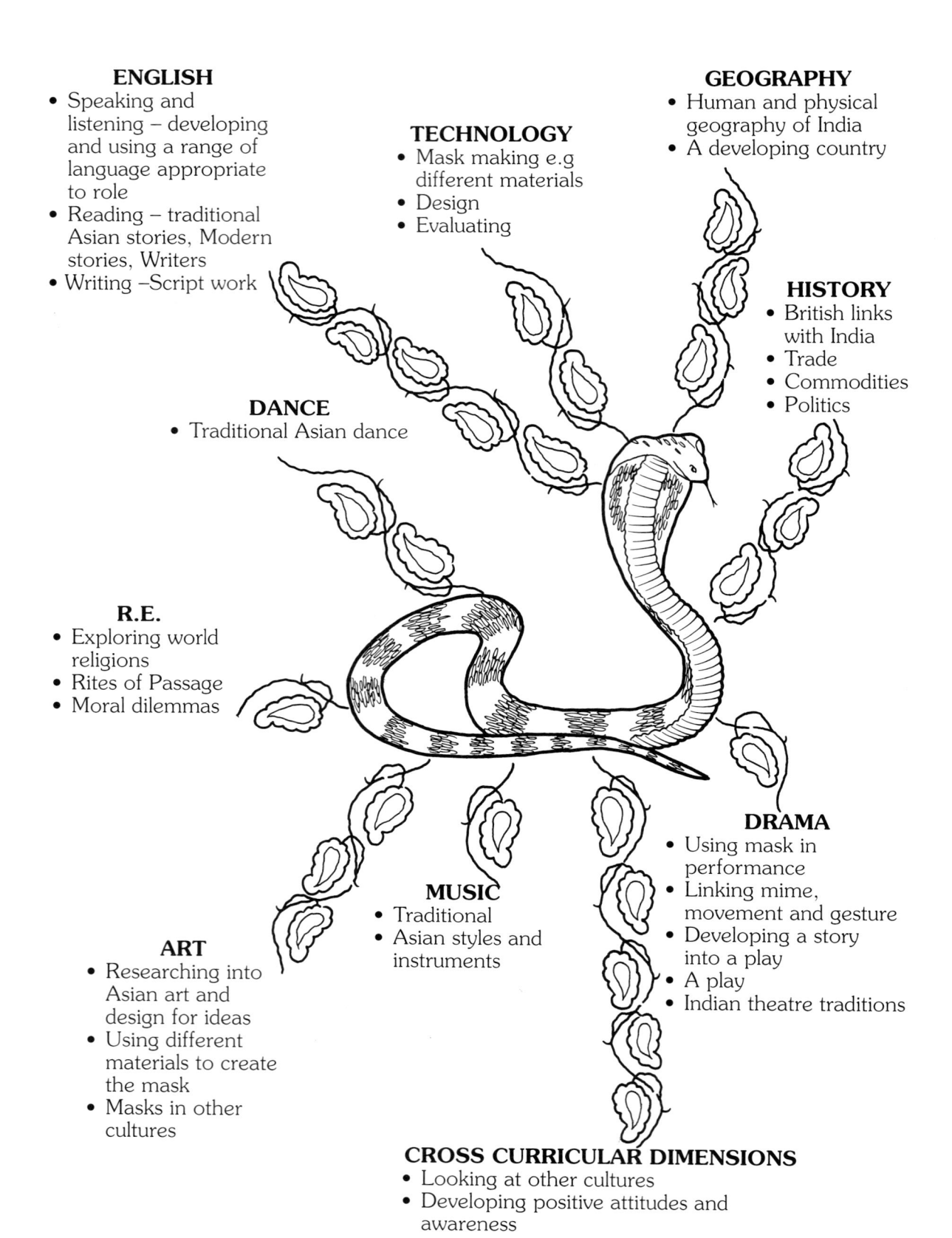

ENGLISH
- Speaking and listening – developing and using a range of language appropriate to role
- Reading – traditional Asian stories, Modern stories, Writers
- Writing – Script work

TECHNOLOGY
- Mask making e.g different materials
- Design
- Evaluating

GEOGRAPHY
- Human and physical geography of India
- A developing country

HISTORY
- British links with India
- Trade
- Commodities
- Politics

DANCE
- Traditional Asian dance

R.E.
- Exploring world religions
- Rites of Passage
- Moral dilemmas

ART
- Researching into Asian art and design for ideas
- Using different materials to create the mask
- Masks in other cultures

MUSIC
- Traditional
- Asian styles and instruments

DRAMA
- Using mask in performance
- Linking mime, movement and gesture
- Developing a story into a play
- A play
- Indian theatre traditions

CROSS CURRICULAR DIMENSIONS
- Looking at other cultures
- Developing positive attitudes and awareness

THE DRAMATIC CURRICULUM

This story is an excellent vehicle for teaching drama for years 4,5 & 6. It can cover:

	Key Stage 2
MAKING	Making a mask. Learning to use a mask effectively. Developing mime and movement skills. Using physical theatre techniques. Exploring different styles e.g. slow motion. Making up a play from a story using improvisation techniques.
PERFORMING	Performing a play to an audience. Performing with a mask. Devising a script in a group. Exploring a range of performance style Using the language of performance.
RESPONDING	Expressing thoughts, feelings and ideas about using masks. Linking their performance work to a wider culture.

CREATING THE STORY

CREATING THE STORY

* FROM STORY INTO DRAMA: a simple editing task
* THE SCENES: a running order and extension ideas
* THE CHARACTERS: extending the story – same drama techniques
* THE SERPENT KING: ways of creating a monster without props
* MASKS: simple techniques
* MAKE-UP: simple hints
* STAGING THE EVENT: extended scene outlines ideas for staging and costume

The story

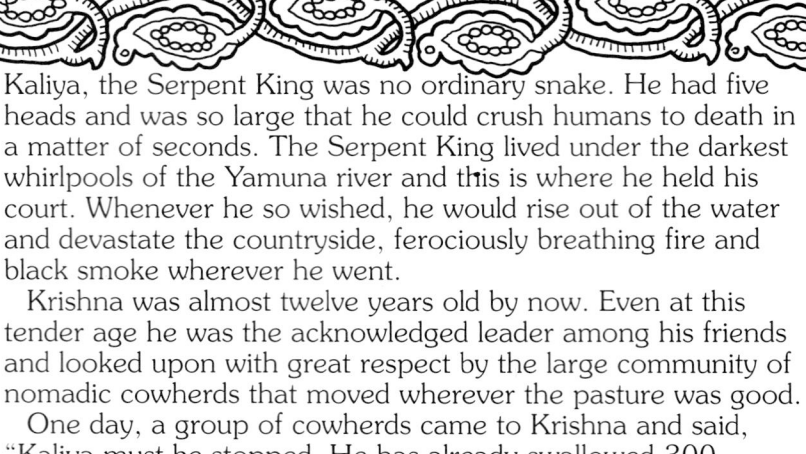

Kaliya, the Serpent King was no ordinary snake. He had five heads and was so large that he could crush humans to death in a matter of seconds. The Serpent King lived under the darkest whirlpools of the Yamuna river and this is where he held his court. Whenever he so wished, he would rise out of the water and devastate the countryside, ferociously breathing fire and black smoke wherever he went.

Krishna was almost twelve years old by now. Even at this tender age he was the acknowledged leader among his friends and looked upon with great respect by the large community of nomadic cowherds that moved wherever the pasture was good.

One day, a group of cowherds came to Krishna and said, "Kaliya must be stopped. He has already swallowed 300 chickens, 178 goats, and 83 cows. Yesterday he killed the blacksmith's son. This is the last straw. Anyone that tries to cross the river, swim, graze cattle, grow watermelons, milk goats or even walk by the river is in danger. Something must be done"

Krishna collected a group of brave friends and walked towards the edge of the water. Suddenly a cloud of black smoke rose above the river, shooting flames swirled upwards and, in one quick swipe, Kaliya encircled all of Krishna's friends in the curl of his body and dragged them down to the bottom of the river.

Having done their dirty deed, the five dreaded heads bobbed up again, breaking the surface of the water. This time the Serpent King was floating along casually, mockingly.

Krishna took one flying leap and landed on all the five hooded heads of the dreaded snake. He crushed one head under one arm and another head under another arm. With his feet he began a heavy-footed dance on the remaining three.

Kaliya felt as if all the mountains of the Himalayas were raining on his head. Such was the power of Krishna's feet.

He decided to dive into his under-water court. He would drown Krishna this way.

Krishna held his breath as Kaliya dived deeper and deeper.

Having killed two of Kaliya's heads Krishna began squeezing the next two under his arm until they gave up and died.

The last head fought on. It snapped and lunged at Krishna and breathed fire on him, but Krishna trapped that head, too, under his arm and began to squeeze.

Kaliya gave a few last gasps and died.

Krishna swam into Kaliya's court where all his friends, now quite pale and blue, lay dying. He pulled them out of the water and laid them down on the shore. Then, with his mouth he breathed life into each one saying, "Dearest friends, it is time to awaken. Kaliya our enemy is dead.

Awaken. Awaken. It is time to tend our cows"

Source: *Seasons of Splendour* by Madhur Jaffrey.
Published by Penguin ISBN 0 14031 854 2

How to Start

(1) Find a suitable story e.g. Serpent King.
(2) Edit story into scenes.
(3) Divide up your class.
(4) Match scenes to class groups.
(5) Create extra scenes if necessary.
(6) Each scene starts as a frozen picture.
(7) Animate each scene if required.
 e.g. bring to life via – movement
 – mime
 – dance
 – music
 – choral speaking
 – dialogue
 – song
 – sounds
(8) Use narrator to link scenes and fill in narrative gaps.
(9) Enhance group work with simple masks or symbolic props/costume, eg a crown.
(10) Rehearse in order.
(11) Present to a suitable audience.
(12) Record the event.

The Scene Order

A possible structure

Scene 1
The village where Krishna lives
A pastoral scene

Scene 2
The underwater Kingdom of Kaliya – the threat of evil

Scene 3
The villagers come to Krishna with their problem they need help

Scene 4
The confrontation,
Krishna versus Kaliya

Scene 5
The rescue

Scene 6
The village celebrates

THE CHARACTERS

Kaliya

Krishna

Cowherds

Brave friends

Additional characters

Villagers

Farm animals

Dancers, musicians

Sea monsters

Kaliya's mother

EXTENSION IDEAS

In order to put the play together, you need to work on each scene with your class – a little at a time.
The easiest approach is to do each scene as STILL IMAGE which has been used many times before, see page 9.

The Strategy

> A still image is an image making technique.
> It is quick.
> It is easy.
> It is controlled.
>
> There is no movement.
> There is no speech.
>
> The picture has to tell the story of the scene.
>
> The bodyshape, gesture, facial expressions, use of pace, use of levels, all combine to give the picture.

The Basic Approach

1. Divide the class into groups of four or five.
2. Set the task– "I want a frozen picture of Krishna at home in his village: a peaceful moment"
3. Give them a strict time limit e.g. 60 seconds.
4. Countdown to the frozen moment – 3,2,1, FREEZE!
4. Give 5 seconds "wriggle time" then freeze
6. Evaluate, review, refine and extend.

The basic approach is used with 5 year olds. For older pupils it is a foundation on which to build further ideas, as listed below.

Extending the image

see Cinderella, page 9

(1) Bring each image to life using mime and movement.
(2) Do it in slow motion.
(3) Do it at double speed.
(4) Each character in the picture speaks one word in turn which reflects their character.
(5) Each character in the picture speaks one word in turn which reflects their feelings.
(6) Each character, in turn, speaks their thoughts.
(7) Each character, in turn, speaks a line of dialogue to tell the story.
(8) The image is brought to life using vocal sounds.
(9) Each image is brought to life by another group providing an instrumental soundtrack.
(10) One or two characters step out of the action to address the audience and comment on the action.
(11) The characters in the image speak as a chorus.
(12) As teacher, step into the image to question individual characters to deepen their understanding.

Creating Kaliya

The image-making approach is a useful technique to get your class to develop one image of Kaliya the 5-headed monster.

Divide them into groups of 5/6. The task – to create, using still image, a five headed monster which is one body with 5 heads. "Use only your bodies – no props."

As groups devise their image, encourage them to use different levels and joining techniques.

Show the images.

Now bring to life using movement.

Add sound.

Share each group and decide (diplomatically) which image will represent Kaliya.

Once an image has been chosen on elements drawn from several groups – get each group to construct the same image.

This time, Kaliya, speaks – the words reveal his true character.

What does Kaliya say?

How does it sound?

Does each head speak individually or as a chorus?

The 5-headed monster

PRODUCTION TECHNIQUES

The Serpent King lends itself to a number of the characters being portrayed through the use of masks

e.g. Kaliya
      sea creatures
      farm animals

● *What is a mask?*

One definition is "something worn to conceal the face; a likeness of a person's face in clay, wax etc; a grotesque representation of a face worn at festive and other occasions to produce a humorous or terrifying effect."

But this definition omits one vital aspect – using a mask enables a person to become another being. The mask signifies that other being in the way it is shaped, adorned and embellished.

It would be useful to show pupils a range of masks from other cultures in order to resource their mask work and deepen their understanding of the theatrical and cultural traditions associated with this technique.

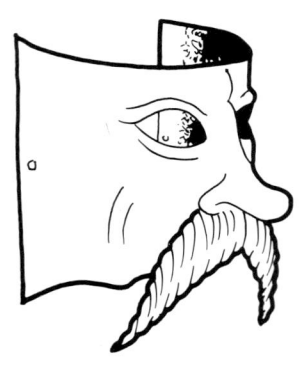

An Italian mask – from Commedia dell 'Arte

North American Indian (Tlinglit) Hawk mask

Ancient Greek terracotta

Japanese Noh mask

A pantomime cat mask

The masks shown opposite, can be complex and expensive to re-create. Remember, the simpler the better and the more effective in the end.

Some simple mask-making techniques

(1) Very effective and secure masks can be made from a simple card framework. This mask leaves the lower half of the face uncovered so the speaker can talk clearly and be heard without muffling.

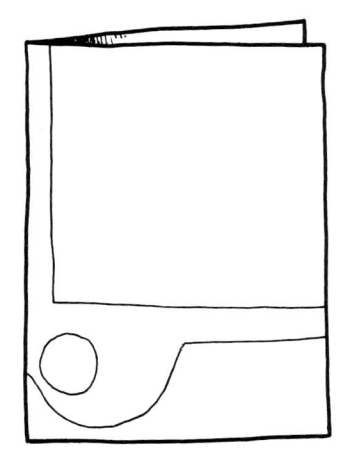

Stage 1
Cut shape out of large piece of folded card and use scraps which remain to embellish basic mask shape

Strengthen joins with masking tape

Stage 2
This bare half mask can now be decorated and embellished with beads, sequins, wool, glitter etc, as well as paint/felt tip

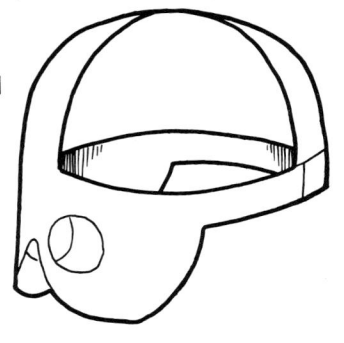

Fasten at the back with strong tape or staple

Stage 3
Child's face covered with fully decorated sea monster face

(2) Cover an inflated balloon with papier-mâché. This is messy, fun and effective. When the structure is bone dry, puncture the balloon carefully. Cut the paper into two sections top and bottom.

Using one section, cut into the required shape.

Cut out the eyes.

Leave a large space for the mouth.

Paint.

When dry, embellish and adorn with glitter; dangly streamers; sequins; floaty material.

This technique needs patience as the newspaper structure, though strong when dry, becomes weak if made too wet.

Strengthen edges with masking tape.

Store carefully on hooks above floor level!

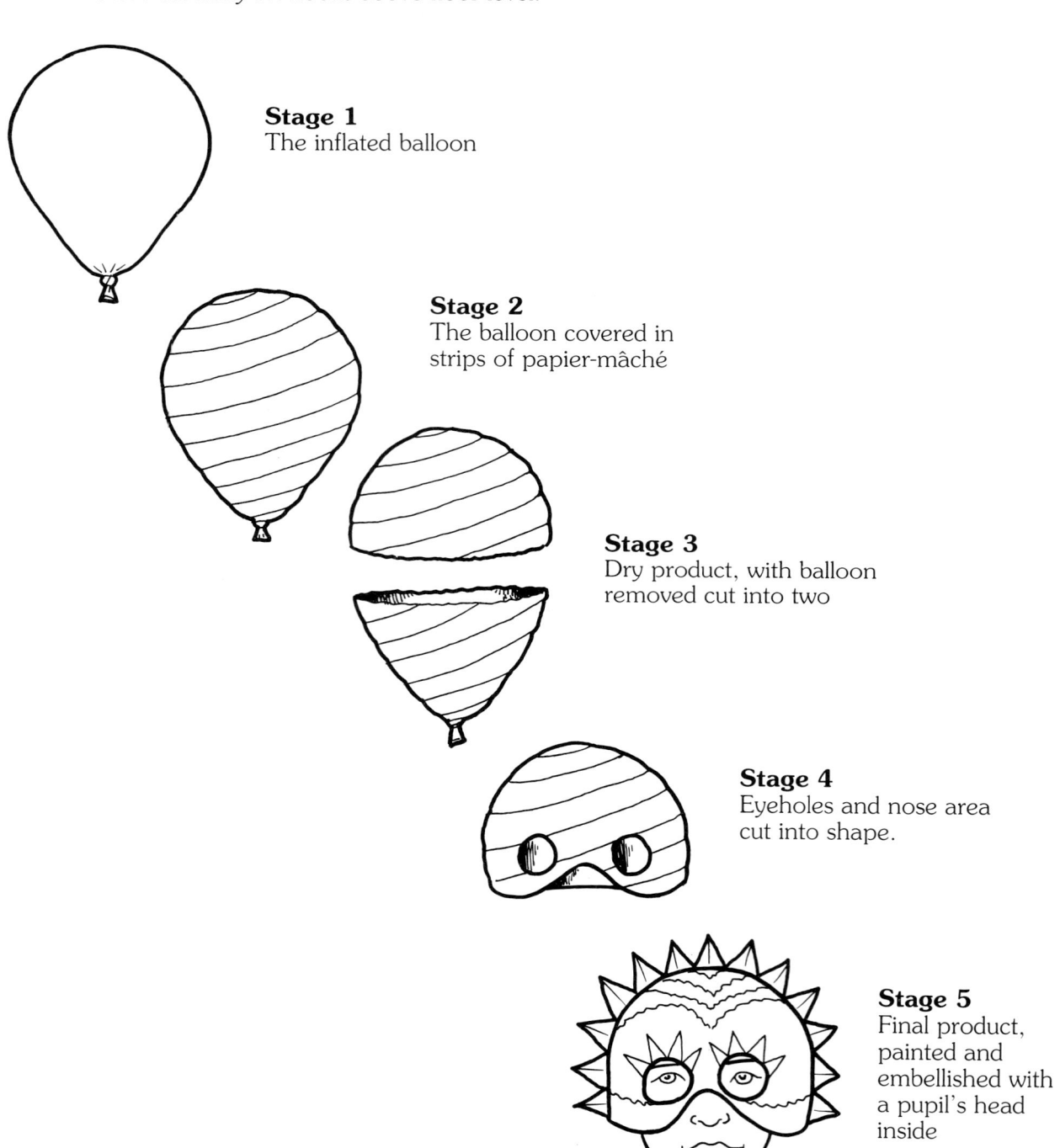

Stage 1
The inflated balloon

Stage 2
The balloon covered in strips of papier-mâché

Stage 3
Dry product, with balloon removed cut into two

Stage 4
Eyeholes and nose area cut into shape.

Stage 5
Final product, painted and embellished with a pupil's head inside

(3) Some more advanced techniques use gummed strip and tissue paper or the ready made bandage which when wet turns into plaster. This is used in hospitals to plaster broken limbs.

(4) Very simple masks can be made from:
* A strong brown paper bag – the type that groceries or garden equipment are carried home in.
  This is cut and decorated.
* A cereal packet – cut, decorated and attached to the pupil's head using elastic.
* Photographs stuck onto card and cut into an appropriate shape
  e.g. a camera
  a car
  a clock
* Simple card, cut, painted and stuck onto a small stick. This is held in front of the face like at a masked ball.

In order to ensure that the masks are effective, the pupils need to explore in their drama lessons
- different movements of the head
- pace of movements – slow and fast
- different movements of the body
- different mouth shapes
- different emotions: can they show fear, joy, anger, happiness effectively?
- how does this character in a mask react to
  Krishna
  Kaliya
  the other creatures?

TIP
When performing the play, remember the most effective mask work occurs when facing the audience, so stage the play "end on" (see Nativity Section, page 26).

Make-up

Do you really need it?

It is important to decide on the use of stage make-up as it is an added expense, time consuming and messy.

The most effective use of stage make-up in school is using simple face paints to create a stunning effect.

Again, as with masks, the simpler, the better.

You can invest in 'greasepaint' as invented by Leichner in 1865. It comes in stick form and a variety of colours and needs to be removed with make-up removal cream.

Greasepaints can be messy and unhygienic. You also need to invest in large quantities of tissues to remove the paint.

Cake make-up is non-greasy and comes in water-based pallets. It is a simpler technique. You can put this on using a dampened sponge. It is water based and so can be washed off.

But both approaches are expensive. Stick with face paints: cheaper, simpler and more effective.

STAGING THE EVENT

Krishna

Kaliya

A villager

Sea creatures

Farm animals

A cowherd

76

The stage

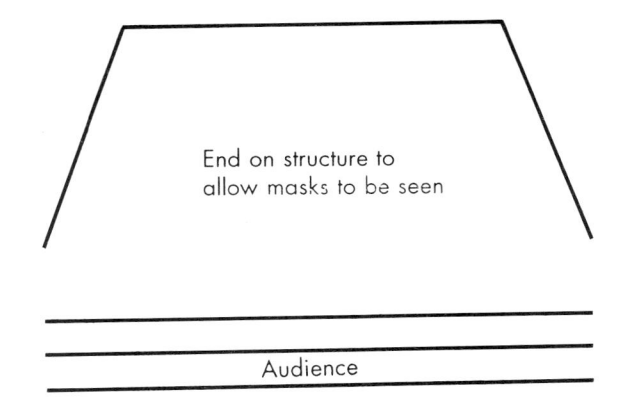

```
End on structure to
allow masks to be seen

Audience
```

Costume

The face masks are the main focus and will draw the audience's attention.
Keep the rest of the costume very simple – T-shirts; polo neck sweaters; tights; leggings.
The sea creatures could add tails from material or hinged card.
They could also wear gloves or wristbands which are embellished with trailing 'seaweed' or other nasty underwater weeds.
Krishna should be easily recognisable – add gold/silver to his/her shirt in the form of a belt/neck band/bracelets.
The simpler the costume, the easier it is to wear, the cheaper it is to make and the more effective it appears to the audience.

Extending the scenes

Start and end each scene with a freeze.

Scene 1   The Pastoral Scene
This scene is to show the village at peace.
   Activities can be bought to life from the initial freeze through careful mime and movement.
Village activities could include:
- feeding the hens
- tending the cows
- fetching water
- making bread
- sweeping the paths
- caring for the crops
- weaving
- carving
- fishing
- grooming horses

Use a narrator to set the scene, to tell the audience the story and then to step into the scene. This enables the narrator to become part of the action and to question villagers about their work.
   The narrator can then "step out" of the action to commentate on the arrival of Krishna, our hero.

At this point, the villagers stop work to cheer their hero.

Scene 2   The Underwater Kingdom
The narrator introduces the evil kingdom of Kaliya – each sea creature, using slow motion movement accompanied by suitable vocal sounds comes to life one by one until the stage area is covered with slithering, wriggling creatures.
   Enter Kaliya, the 5-headed monster who parades around the stage finally addressing the audience and telling them of his evil deeds.

Each head could speak in turn.
Head 1. "300 chickens
Head 2. 178 goats
Head 3. 83 cows
Head 4. 1 blacksmith's son
Head 5. and I am still hungry"

The monster could then speak as a chorus.
   "I am Kaliya
   King of the river
   I am the mighty one
   The underwater master
   Slithery, slimy, silky and supreme."

Scene 3 : The Villagers come to Krishna

This scene can be played with straight dialogue.

The first part of the scene depicts the villagers discussing their problem.

The second part is the approach to Krishna and request for help.

The final part is where Krishna states his plan and gathers brave friends together to go to the river.

Try improvising the scene first. Make sure the pupils understand the content of each section.

In the early stages, give each pupil a number so that they can speak one line in order.

This helps them to focus and stops one pupil becoming too dominant. Once they have this initial dialogue sorted and memorised, they can develop their dialogue.

Encourage them to write down their lines. They will begin to develop a script to which they can all contribute.

Scene 4 : The Confrontation

This is a fight sequence. Fights in drama can be problematic as well as disruptive and dangerous.

The best approach is through using slow motion and giving the pupils a framework i.e. a set number of moves such as 5 attacking blows and 5 defending blows.

By giving the slow motion structure, the fight is defused and moves into stylised dance.

In this scene, the brave friends come to grief first watched by the sea creatures.

Then Krishna appears and slowly one by one immobilises the heads. The fifth and final head lasts the longest but finally bows to Krishna's superior strength.

You could use the narrator as a commentator or small groups of pupils – as villagers could comment on the action in chorus.

Use suitable music – either a pre-recorded piece or live percussion composed by the pupils.

A slow motion dance fight accompanied by live percussion interspaced with chorus style comments are the ingredients for a dramatic scene.

Scene 5 : The Rescue

This scene merges with scene 4 – the style of performance can be altered by the thoughts of the dying friends being spoken aloud and echoed by the audience.

Krishna breathes life into his companions and they are dragged from the river by anxious villagers.

Krishna emerges last of all carrying a memento of Kaliya e.g. a crown.

The villagers cheer and hoist Krishna aloft to carry him in triumph to the village for a celebration.

Scene 6 : The Celebration

This scene is an opportunity to perform music and dance which reflects aspects of traditional Indian performing arts that the pupils have researched and composed .

Finally, Krishna accepts garlands and gifts from his villagers.

The narrator can step into the action and interview Krishna. The interview could be interrupted by the arrival of a strange woman.

"I am looking for my son
His name is Kaliya
I am his mother
It is his birthday
I have a gift for him
Where can I find him?"

You can end on the celebration or you could extend the drama by adding this moral dilemma.

You could ask your audience for advice and then act out the agreed ending. This is risky but highly dramatic and can stimulate heated discussion on moral issues such as:

Did Kaliya deserve to die?

How else could Krishna have dealt with Kaliya?

End note

The story is a traditional tale from India with violent elements wrapped up in a moral tale of good triumphing over evil. The violent aspects of the story need to be discussed in order to highlight the modern approaches to violent action in our society. "How else could Krishna have dealt with Kaliya"? is an important question to discuss in detail so as to explore non-violent approaches to a difficult problem.

RESOURCES

The Complete Book of Paper Mask Making Michael Grater, Dover ISBN 0 4862 47120

Seasons of Splendour by Madhur Jaffrey, Penguin ISBN 0 14031 8542

Costume For the Stage Sheila Jackson ISBN 0 9069 6977 8

Designing and Making Costumes Motley, Herbert Press ISBN 1 8715 6944 3

Make-up Kits Available from major outlets including
– AJS, Tel: 01425 470888.
– Benn Nye: stage, film and make-up equipment plus a range of videos.
– Leichner: traditional British theatical make-up range.
– Kryolan Brandel: a long established German company, produces a range of make-up.

Craftpacks, 25 Hunts Pond Road, Titchfield Common, FAREHAM PO14 4PJ lots of useful bits and pieces for decoration and make-up. Ask for a catalogue.

THE SHADOW PUPPET PROJECT

A traditional Balinese puppet

INTRODUCTION

Have you ever used your hands to make:
- *birds wings, flapping in flight*
- *a rabbit's face, ears and eye that moves*
- *a monster with a snapping jaw*

All against a sunny wall?

If you have, then you can quickly learn to make and use shadow puppets.

The origins of shadow puppets began over 2000 years ago in the East. Some believe it began in China, others see the roots of this style of theatre in India, Egypt and Indonesia. Each country developed its own individual style. The connecting thread was that, in each case, the puppets acted out religious or mystical tales.

Shadow puppetry is still an important art form in many Eastern countries today particularly in Indonesia. Balinese stick puppets can be found today in many shops or as wall decorations.

Originally these puppets were made from leather and decorated with intricate patterns cut out from the material.

They were often dyed and oiled so that they could stand out behind a lighted screen. Wooden sticks were attached to manipulate the puppets. These intricate characters would then act out events taken from 'The Mahabarata' or 'The Ramayana'. The puppet master would chant the story, manipulate the puppets, direct the music and create the sound effects. Performances could last as long as a night.

The music would be percussion based and the stories always revolving around good and evil.

The shadow puppet plays you could create can be simple, effective, cheap and give pupils of all abilities a sense of achievement. This project is particularly successful with pupils who have special learning difficulties.

All the pupils gain a sense of awe and wonder as they re-create an ancient theatrical tradition in their own style.

This is an easy project to do.

All age ranges and abilities can be highly successful with this art form. Some of the most effective and startling work I have witnessed has been performed by pupils with learning difficulties and a range of physical disabilities.

Ideas for stories which can be acted out as shadow plays are offered and a well known nursery rhyme is described in detail to help you plan and execute your own project.

The methods for making a range of creatures and people is also given, with the emphasis being on simplicity and accessibility for all ages and abilities.

Production and staging techniques are covered including how to make a shadow screen, plus lighting techniques and ideas for experimenting with different materials to create special effects.

It is a highly effective, simple and satisfying technique. Try it out and you'll be surprised at the simple techniques which create stunning effects!

Shadow puppets are a good framework because:

They are eye catching

They are easy to make

You do not need special equipment

It explores traditional theatre from another culture

It is a simple but highly effective storytelling technique

Pupils of all abilities can take part

Any story – old or new – can be used

They're cheap!

This technique covers many aspects of the core and foundation curriculum

It helps pupils to work as a team

It is a good way of developing storytelling skills

Percussion can be added to enhance the story

CURRICULAR LINKS

HISTORY
- Historical background of puppets
- Uses in history e.g. Jack O'Lantern in Victorian times

DRAMA
- People as puppets
- Story into puppet play
- Mime and movement
- Lighting

ENGLISH
- Styles of narrative
- Oral tradition
- Storytelling to accompany shadow plays
- Puppets in the media e.g. Spitting Image

ART
- Investigating shadow puppets from other cultures
- Making puppets from a range of materials
- Modifying designs through performance

SCIENCE
- Exploring different uses of light and light sources
- Using colour for effects
- Sound

GEOGRAPHY
- Cultural use of puppets in Asia

MUSIC
- Composing pieces for the play
- Using different instruments
- Performing or recording the piece

TECHNOLOGY
- Identifying needs of making a puppet
- Designing the puppet
- Making it from different materials
- Evaluating its use through performance

R.E.
- Stories with moral content e.g. good versus evil
- Puppets in religion e.g. Hinduism

DANCE
- Combining human movement and a puppet
- Studying movements

THE DRAMATIC CURRICULUM

Using shadow puppets supports exciting areas of the dramatic curriculum at KS1 and KS2.

	Key Stage 1	**Key Stage 2**
MAKING	Making a shadow puppet. Learning to manipulate their puppet. Creating moving joints through simple fixings Creating a story and using their puppet to tell it to an audience. Using their voices to tell their story.	Developing and making shadow puppets with complex joints. Creating the story for their puppets. Developing a script. Using highlighting and sound. Incorporating some dramatic conventions into their play e.g. puppets speaking thoughts aloud.
PERFORMING	Taking part in a group play. Telling story to an audience. Performing with a puppet and using special techniques.	Taking part in a group play as a puppeteer, narrator, musician or technician. Communicating their play effectively to an audience. with technical effects.
RESPONDING	Saying how it felt to take part in a shadow play. Discussing the use of the puppets and how it felt to use them.	Evaluating their work and discussing improvements. Relating their puppet play to other styles from other cultures.

CREATING THE STORY

Shadow puppet plays lend themselves to exploring a range of traditional western stories and classic tales from eastern culture.

It is useful to have a range of stories available so pupils can research and discover new ideas.

Some successful ideas which have been adapted to shadow plays are:

* Traditional Nursery Rhymes
  e.g. Humpty Dumpty
  Hickory, Dickory Dock
  Mary, Mary, Quite Contrary.
* Traditional Western Stories
  e.g. Pandora's Box
  Aesops Fables
  Jack and The Beanstalk
  Beowulf
  Anansi
* Classic Tales from the East
  e.g. The Mahabarta
  The Ramayana
  Chinese Dragon Tales
* Aborigine Tales
  e.g. The First Sunrise
* Tales from the Bible
  e.g. The Good Samaritan

Any story can be adapted, even stories based on the plays of Shakespeare. The essence of a traditional shadow puppet play is the emphasis on morality and traditional religious teachings.

A more varied approach could be achieved by encouraging the pupils to adapt a piece of their creative writing into a shadow puppet play. This encourages drafting and editing skills as well as exploring script writing techniques. Pupils will have a real purpose for their plays.

If a simpler technique is more applicable, pupils do not always need a story. They can simply use the shadow puppets to create a scene such as a jungle, a butterfly farm, an underwater sequence. These scenes when accompanied by appropriate music are very effective and easy to create.

PRODUCTION TECHNIQUES

Making a screen

You will need: a drama screen (see Nativity Project, page 27)
a white cotton sheet
staples
staple gun

The drama screen is a versatile piece of equipment and is perfect for use in this project.

Set up the screen.

Cover the side panels with black card or paper. These can become the "wings" or offstage area for the puppeteers to await their cue.

Remove the horizontal bars from the central panel and store safely.
This is now an empty panel.

Cut to size a cotton white sheet to fit the central panel.

Cover the central panel and fix the sheet tightly using staples. Do make sure it is taut.

You now have a screen.

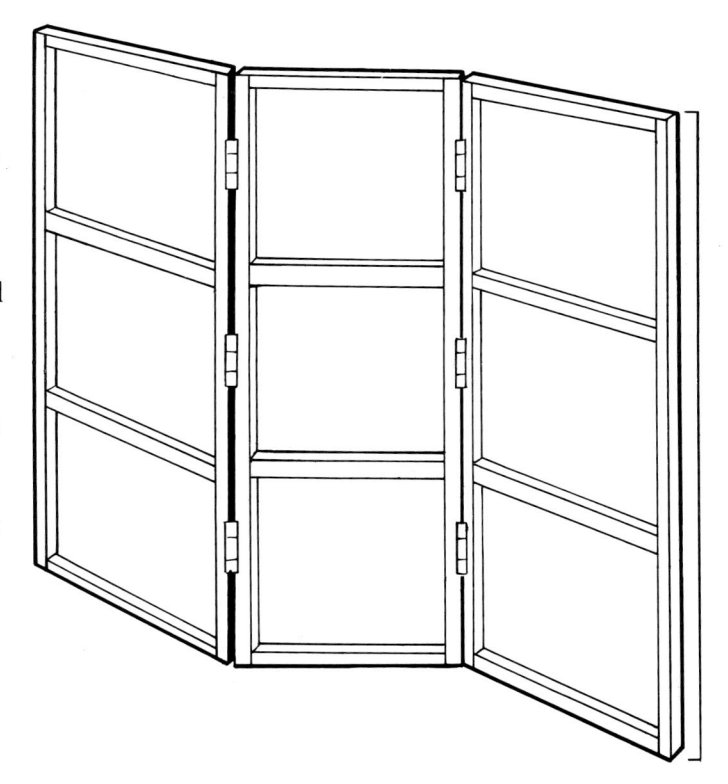

Lighting the screen

You will need :

(1) One slide projector raised on stand to project a strong beam of light onto the back of the screen.
    Special effects could be achieved by the use of coloured slides.

(2) An overhead projector can also be used. This has a powerful beam too.

(3) A parcan stage lantern can also be used, or a fresnel or spot. They must be safely attached on a stand with any cable securely fixed.

Do try to position the light source so it projects only onto the screen and not onto walls or ceilings.

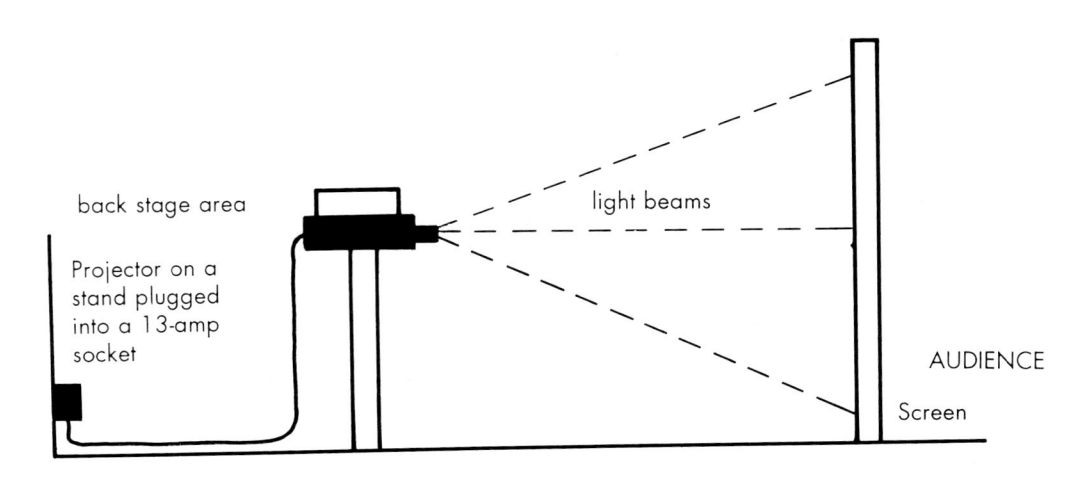

Try experimenting with:
- Coloured slides in the projector or gels in the stage lanterns.
- Torch beams.
- Lace or cake doilies.
- String or sequin lengths attached to a puppet.
- A small pot plant placed in front of the light source becomes a jungle!
- Glass bottles.
- Boxes with objects coming in and out.
- Human body shapes.
- 3D objects e.g. cubes made from greaseproof paper.
- Overhead projector and its beam of light.

PERFORMANCE HINTS

It can be fun to see the puppeteer in action especially if he/she interacts with the puppet.

There may be stories where the puppeteer must not be seen. A table or PE bench turned on its side against the screen gives the effect of a ledge or stage. This gives a puppeteer a barrier to work behind and a stage for the puppet to perform on.

Care: make sure any table legs are covered in cloth so puppeteers do not hurt themselves if they have to move quickly.

Objects can go in and out of puppets. Try it out, it's lots of fun.
e.g. a whale can swallow a fish
    a bird can swallow a worm
    a Venus fly trap plant can swallow a human.
or vice versa!

The story of "The old woman who swallowed a fly" is good for this technique.

Narration : it is best not to have voices coming from behind the screen. The puppeteers have enough to do without doing the dialogue too. The narrator should be in front of the screen so that he/she can be heard clearly and can see the action to time their speeches and link with the puppets.

Musicians : if there is live music, musicians also need to be in front of the screen.

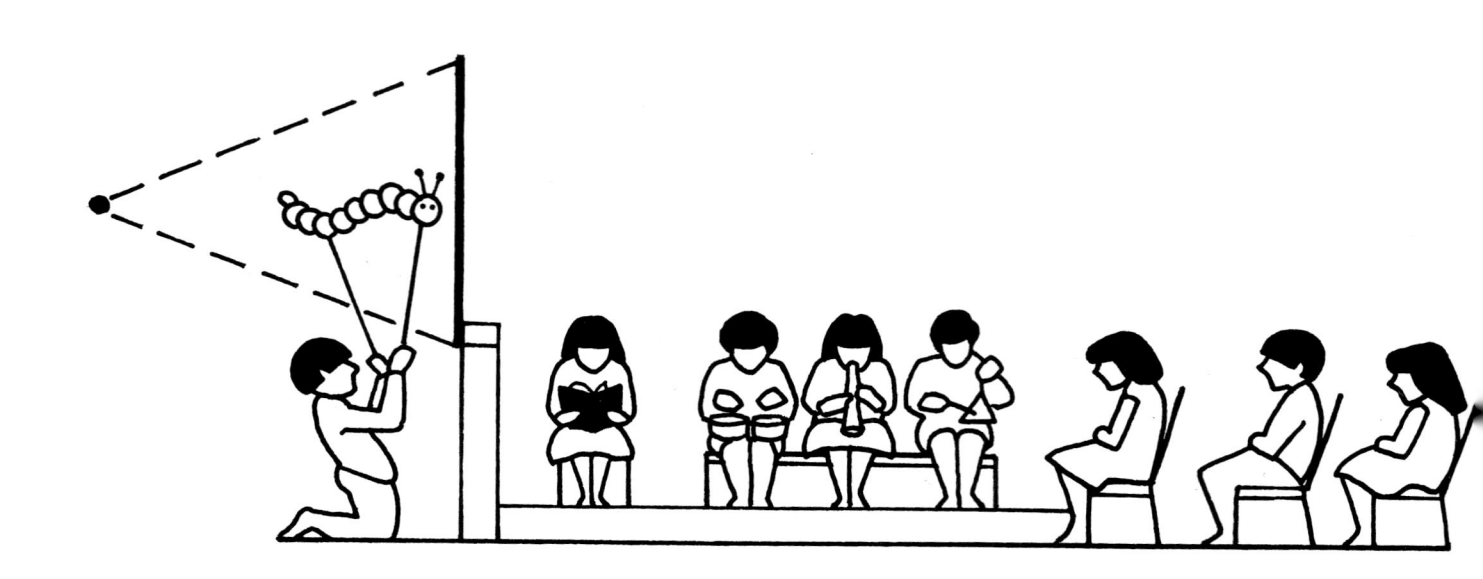

Making a Puppet

You will need :
  Card – any size, any colour
  Sharp scissors
  A hole punch
  String
  Masking tape
  Paper fasteners (butterfly type)
  Paper – for designs
  Varying lengths of bamboo cane or dowelling or garden/plant canes to become the rods to manipulate the puppet.
  Coloured tissue paper
  Coloured cellophane
  Sequin waste
  Bits of lace, gauze or floaty material
  Beads

Stage 1
The design: draw your puppet onto a sheet of paper.
Decide and mark the moving joints
e.g. a frog.

Moving joint

Stage 2
On card, draw the puppet again.
The moving limbs need to be drawn with rounded edges and kept separate.

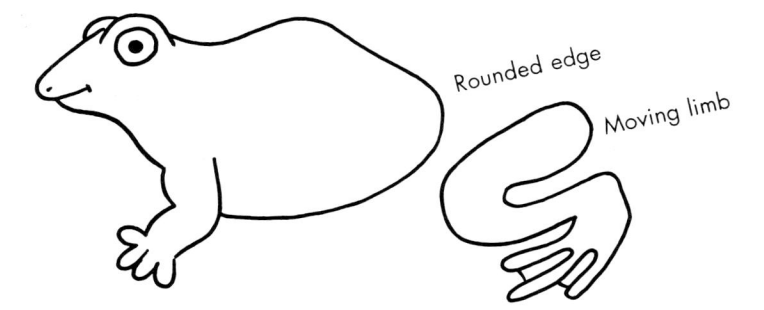

Rounded edge
Moving limb

Stage 3
Using a paper fastener, attach the moving limb to the body. Ensure the brass head of the fastener faces the screen.

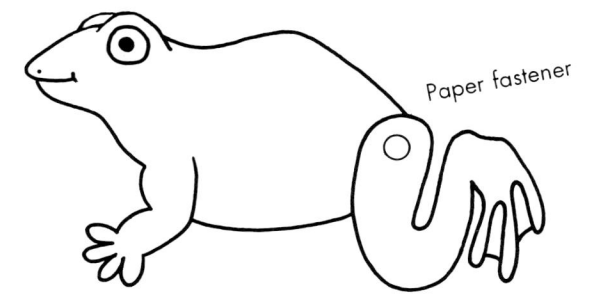

Paper fastener

Stage 4
Attach the rods. You will need 2, one onto the body of the frog and one onto the moving limb.
Use masking tape to attach the rods.
Try to create a strong attachment – trial and error helps here!

Rods attached to frog

Stage 5
The frog is now ready to leap. Place the front of the frog onto the screen. Stand behind and by manipulating the rods, make it leap.
Get a friend to watch from the audience and tell you how it looks.

Stage 6
Storage: lay the frog on a table with the body and limb hanging over the edge and the rods flat on the table. This prevents the card from being damaged.

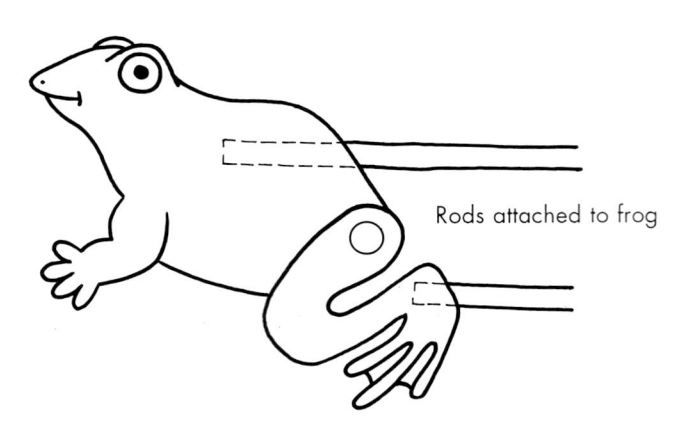

TIP
Birds, animals, fish, insects and mermaids make ideal shadow puppets.

● *Some more ideas for shadow puppets*

(1) A butterfly

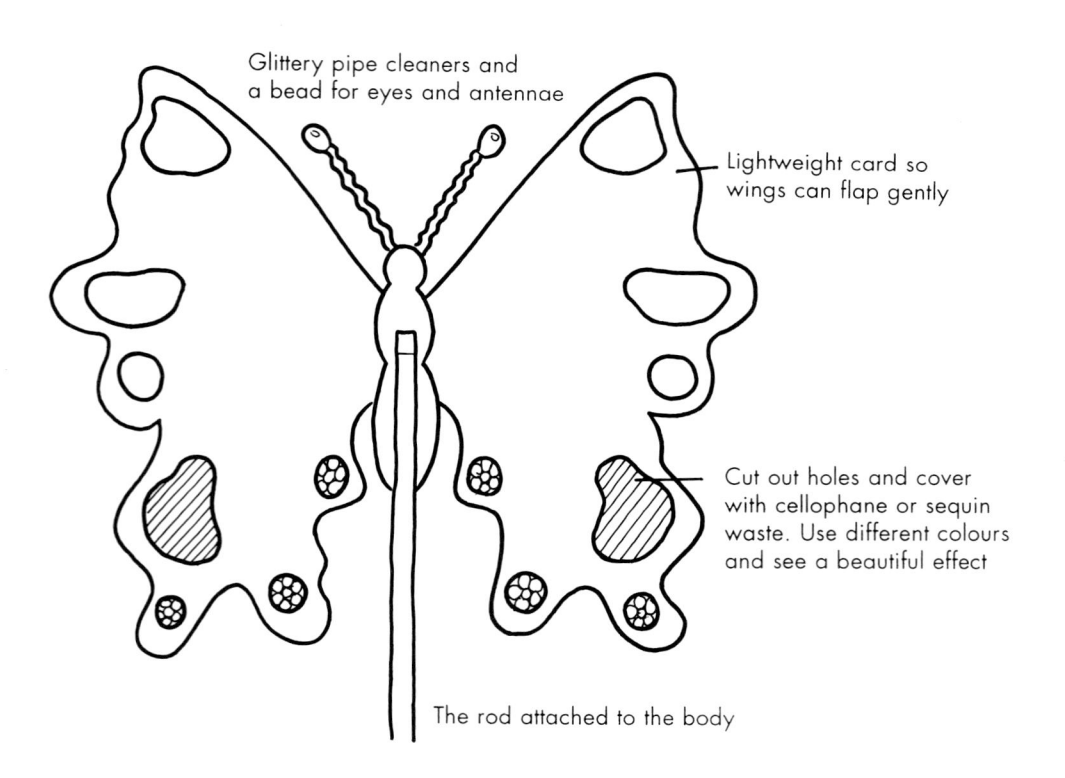

Glittery pipe cleaners and a bead for eyes and antennae

Lightweight card so wings can flap gently

Cut out holes and cover with cellophane or sequin waste. Use different colours and see a beautiful effect

The rod attached to the body

(2) A cat

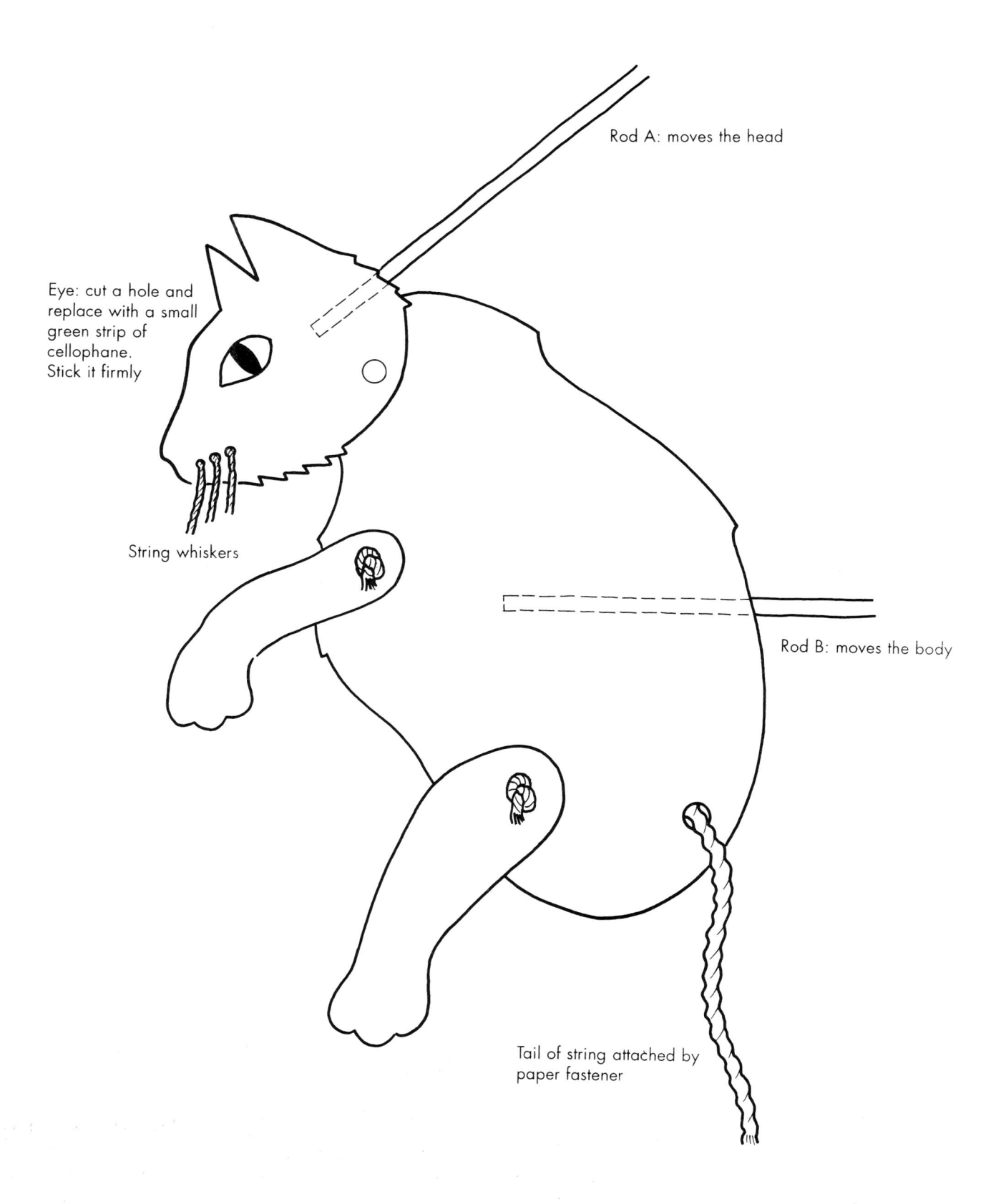

Rod A: moves the head

Eye: cut a hole and replace with a small green strip of cellophane. Stick it firmly

String whiskers

Rod B: moves the body

Tail of string attached by paper fastener

(3) The hungry caterpillar

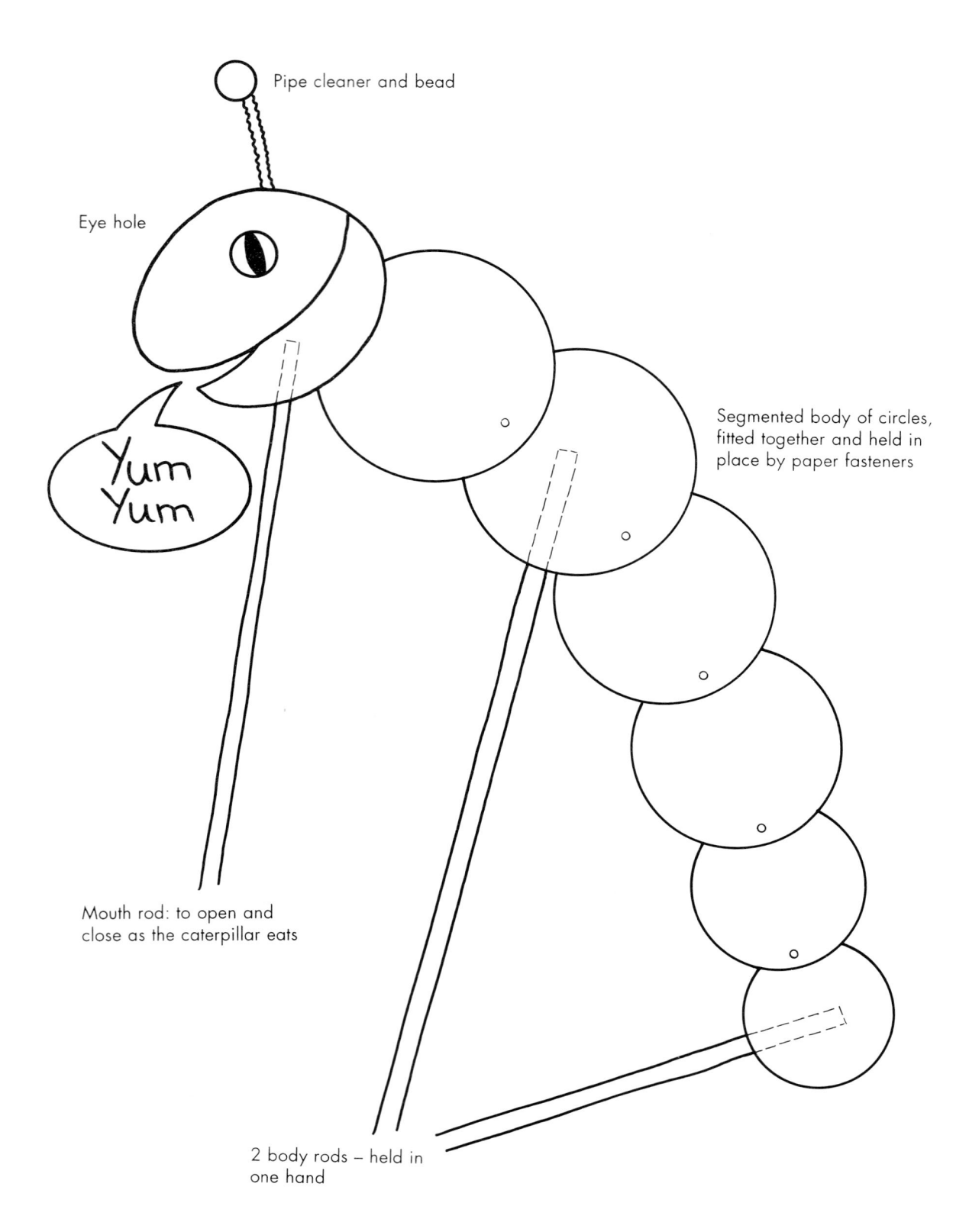

Pipe cleaner and bead

Eye hole

Yum Yum

Segmented body of circles, fitted together and held in place by paper fasteners

Mouth rod: to open and close as the caterpillar eats

2 body rods – held in one hand

(4) Humpty Dumpty

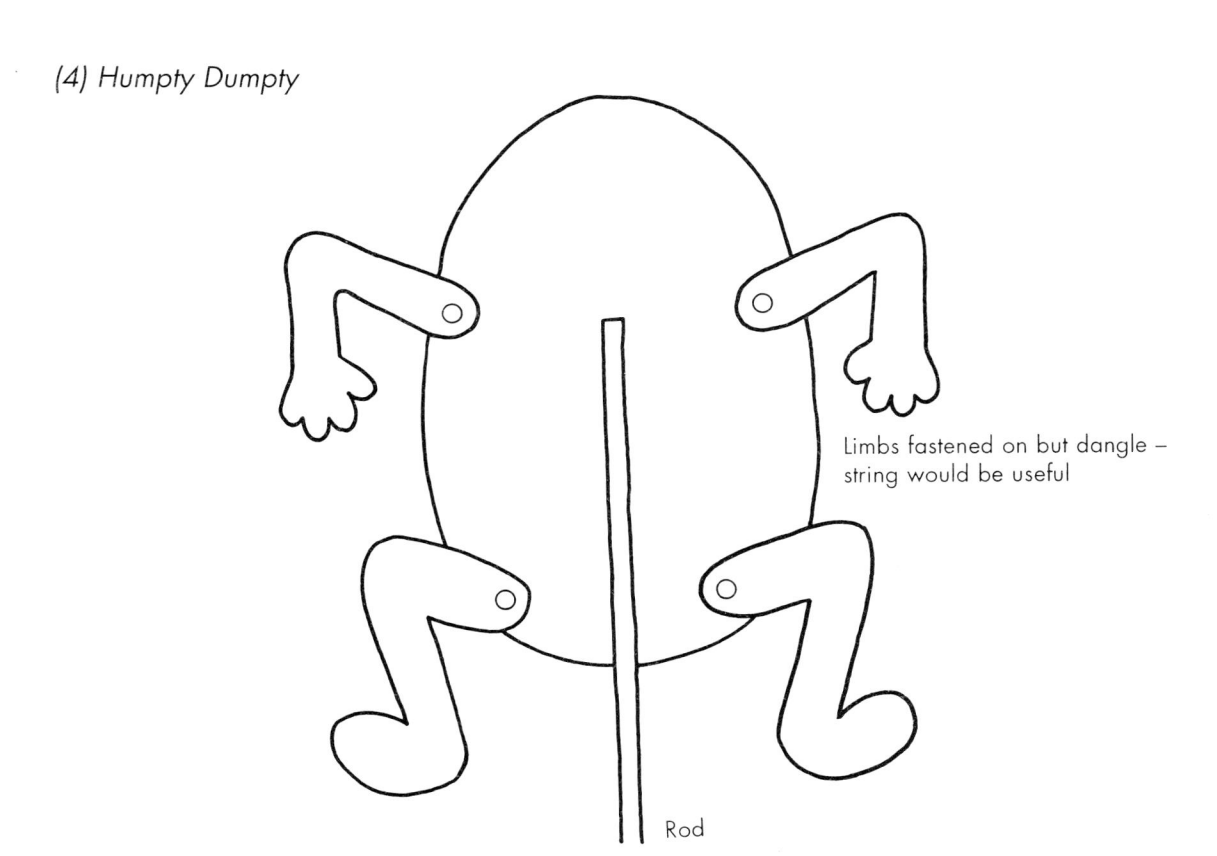

Limbs fastened on but dangle – string would be useful

Rod

Humpty Dumpty had a great fall

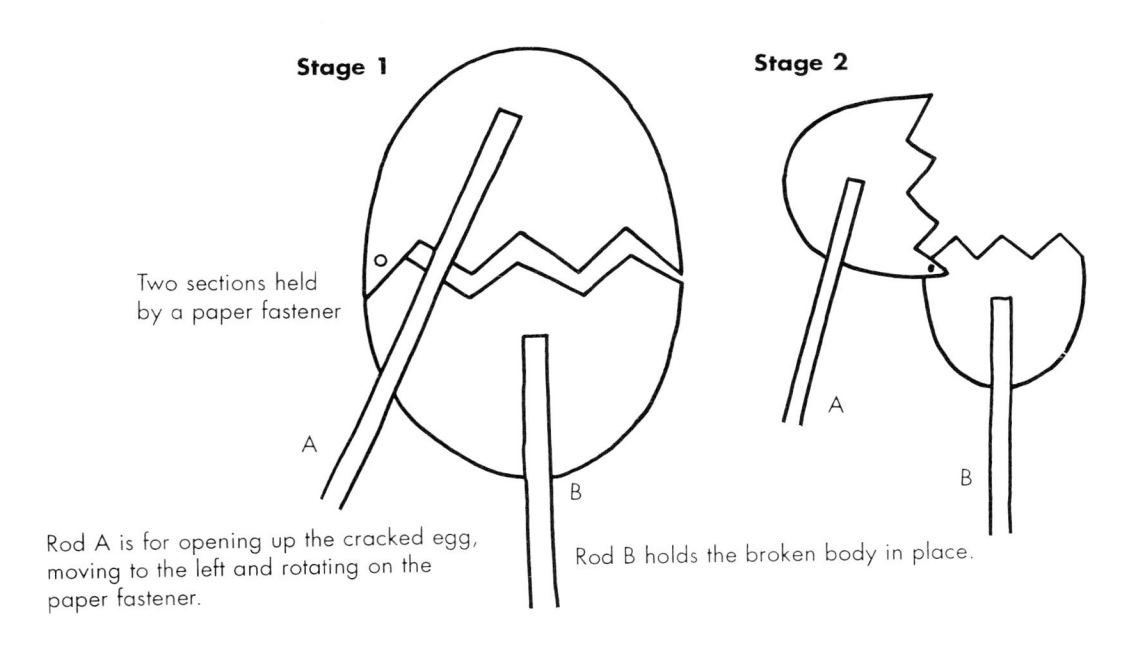

Stage 1

Two sections held by a paper fastener

Rod A is for opening up the cracked egg, moving to the left and rotating on the paper fastener.

Stage 2

Rod B holds the broken body in place.

STAGING THE EVENT

Mary, Mary, Quite Contrary

The screen: the audience's view	Puppets	Script: using a narrator chorus
	Bird Butterfly Cat Mouse Tree	Mary, Mary, quite contrary
	Tree Butterfly Bird Mary and watering can	How does your garden grow?
	Tree Bird Butterfly Mary Flowers	With silver bells
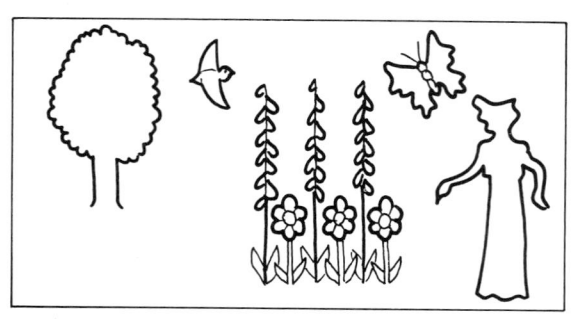	As above but with more flowers	And cockleshells
	Mary, cat, dog, tree bird, butterfly and a garden of beautiful flowers	And pretty maids all in a row

ORGANISING YOUR PERFORMANCE

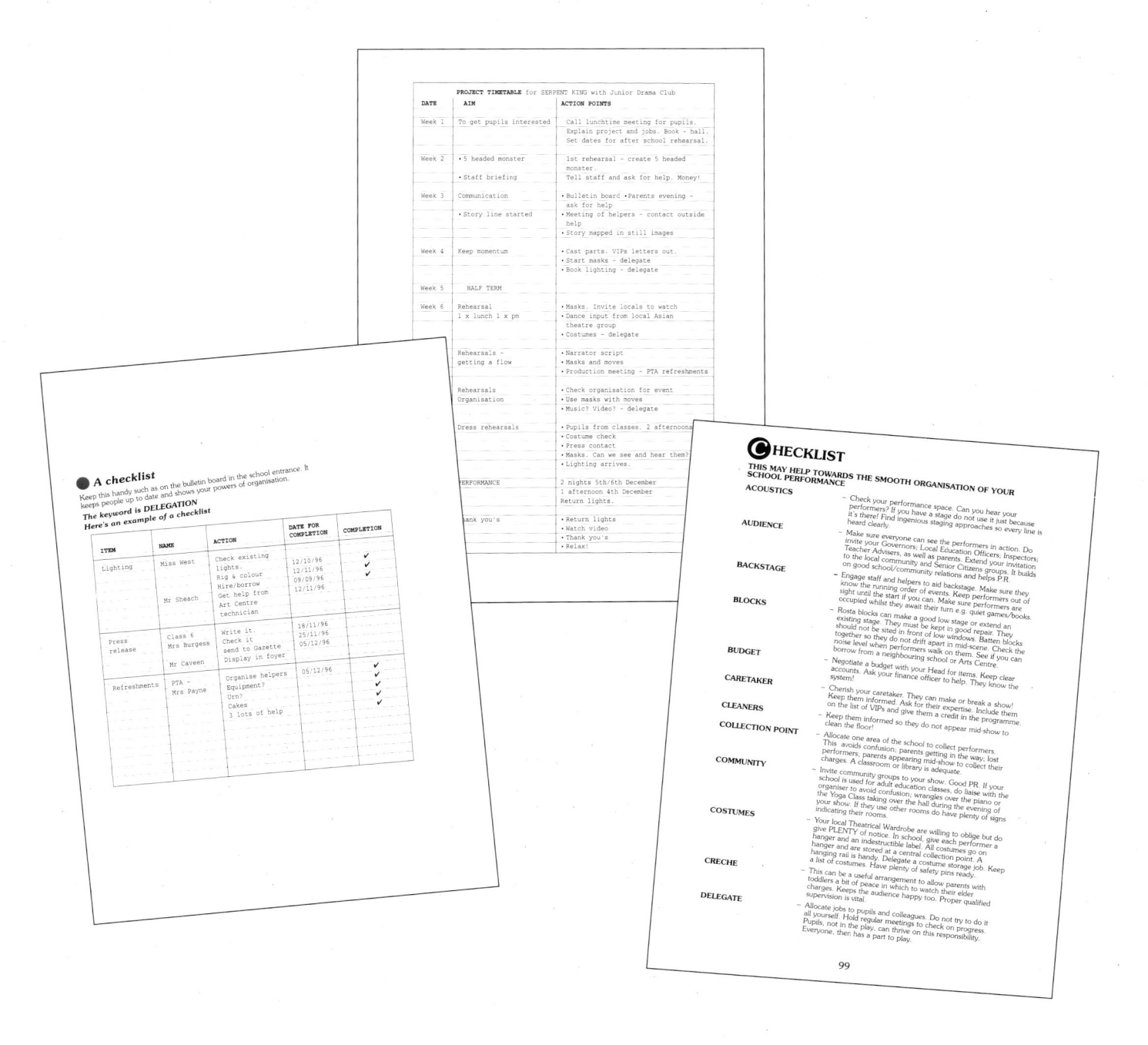

PROJECT TIMETABLE for SERPENT KING with Junior Drama Club

DATE	AIM	ACTION POINTS
Week 1	To get pupils interested	Call lunchtime meeting for pupils. Explain project and jobs. Book - hall. Set dates for after school rehearsal.
Week 2	• 5 headed monster • Staff briefing	1st rehearsal - create 5 headed monster. Tell staff and ask for help. Money!
Week 3	Communication • Story line started	• Bulletin board • Parents evening - ask for help • Meeting of helpers - contact outside help • Story mapped in still images
Week 4	Keep momentum	• Cast parts. VIPs letters out. • Start masks - delegate • Book lighting - delegate
Week 5	HALF TERM	
Week 6	Rehearsal 1 x lunch 1 x pm	• Masks. Invite locals to watch • Dance input from local Asian theatre group • Costumes - delegate
	Rehearsals - getting a flow	• Narrator script • Masks and moves • Production meeting - PTA refreshments
	Rehearsals Organisation	• Check organisation for event • Use masks with moves • Music? Video? - delegate
	Dress rehearsals	• Pupils from classes. 2 afternoons • Costume check • Press contact • Masks. Can we see and hear them? • Lighting arrives.
	PERFORMANCE	2 nights 5th/6th December 1 afternoon 4th December Return lights.
	Thank you's	• Return lights • Watch video • Thank you's • Relax!

● A checklist

Keep this handy such as on the bulletin board in the school entrance. It keeps people up to date and shows your powers of organisation.

The keyword is DELEGATION

Here's an example of a checklist

ITEM	NAME	ACTION	DATE FOR COMPLETION	COMPLETION
Lighting	Miss West Mr Sheach	Check existing lights. Rig & colour Hire/borrow Get help from Art Centre technician	12/10/96 12/11/96 09/09/96 12/11/96	✓ ✓
Press release	Class 6 Mrs Burgess Mr Caveen	Write it. Check it send to Gazette Display in foyer	18/11/96 25/11/96 05/12/96	
Refreshments	PTA - Mrs Payne	Organise helpers Equipment? Urn? Cakes 3 lots of help	05/12/96	✓ ✓ ✓ ✓

● CHECKLIST

THIS MAY HELP TOWARDS THE SMOOTH ORGANISATION OF YOUR SCHOOL PERFORMANCE

ACOUSTICS – Check your performance space. Can you hear your performers? If you have a stage do not use it just because it's there! Find ingenious staging approaches so every line is heard clearly.

AUDIENCE – Make sure everyone can see the performers in action. Do invite your Governors; Local Education Officers; Inspectors; Teacher Advisers, as well as parents. Extend your invitation to the local community and Senior Citizens groups. It builds on good school/community relations and helps P.R.

BACKSTAGE – Engage staff and helpers to aid backstage. Make sure they know the running order of events. Keep performers out of sight until the start if you can. Make sure performers are occupied whilst they await their turn e.g. quiet games/books.

BLOCKS – Rosta blocks can make a good low stage or extend an existing stage. They must be kept in good repair. They should not be sited in front of low windows. Batten blocks together so they do not drift apart in mid-scene. Check the noise level when performers walk on them. See if you can borrow from a neighbouring school or Arts Centre.

BUDGET – Negotiate a budget with your Head for items. Keep clear accounts. Ask your finance officer to help. They know the system!

CARETAKER – Cherish your caretaker. They can make or break a show! Keep them informed. Ask for their expertise. Include them on the list of VIPs and give them a credit in the programme.

CLEANERS – Keep them informed so they do not appear mid-show to clean the floor!

COLLECTION POINT – Allocate one area of the school to collect performers. This avoids confusion; parents getting in the way; lost performers; parents appearing mid-show to collect their charges. A classroom or library is adequate.

COMMUNITY – Invite community groups to your show. Good PR. If your school is used for adult education classes, do liaise with the organiser to avoid confusion; wrangles over the piano or the Yoga Class taking over the hall during the evening of your show. If they use other rooms do have plenty of signs indicating their rooms.

COSTUMES – Your local Theatrical Wardrobe are willing to oblige but do give PLENTY of notice. In school, give each performer a hanger and an indestructible label. All costumes go on hanger and are stored at a central collection point. A hanging rail is handy. Delegate a costume storage job. Keep a list of costumes. Have plenty of safety pins ready.

CRECHE – This can be a useful arrangement to allow parents with toddlers a bit of peace in which to watch their elder charges. Keeps the audience happy too. Proper qualified supervision is vital.

DELEGATE – Allocate jobs to pupils and colleagues. Do not try to do it all yourself. Hold regular meetings to check on progress. Pupils, not in the play, can thrive on this responsibility. Everyone, then has a part to play.

99

93

INTRODUCTION

This chapter gives plenty of practical tips and handy hints for the organisation and smooth running of your event. It is divided into:
1. Roles and responsibilities
2. Budgeting
3. Timetable
4. A checklist to help the smooth running of the event

Organisation, planning, preparation, communication, delegation and enjoyment are the key words. Without them, the task becomes daunting and stressful.

A performance in a school, can be a wonderful, enjoyable and tear-jerking event which affects pupils, teachers, parents and support staff.

It must not be a chore but something you want to do to enrich the social, moral, spiritual and cultural dimensions of the school.

Keep it stress free – the key word is ORGANISATION.

ROLES AND RESPONSIBILITIES

It is important to be clear about who does what in the performance and everyone must be kept informed. This will help to ensure that tasks are completed. People feel happy to help so long as they know exactly what is expected of them.

If you allocate a job, make sure the person knows exactly what to do. Then you will have peace of mind to know that another little worry has been delegated into safe hands.

The key word is: COMMUNICATION.
Here are a few ideas.

● *A typical list of who does what*

Serpent King Project

Director	: Mrs Davies – class 4 teacher
Stage Manager	: Mrs Burgess – class 6 teacher Ruth Taylor – class 6 Jack Morris – class 6
Front of House	: Mrs Knights – headteacher Mr Black – classroom assistant
Masks and Make-up	: Mr Jolly and class 5 (technology topic)
Props	: Sheila Boniface – parent Kevin and Emma Boniface
Costumes	: Bunyard family
Sound and Music	: Year 10 GCSE drama & music pupils from West Hampshire College
Refreshments	: PTA – Mrs Payne (Governor)
Finance, Tickets and Admin	: Office staff plus Mr Waring (admin. officer)
Signs, Seating Parking, and Cleaning	: Mrs Buckingham – caretaker and her husband

Press release and	: Class 6 (English topic) – Mr Caveen
Programmes	
Video	: Year 1 media group – West Hampshire College (Mr Waring to contact)
Photographs	: Mr Buckingham (parent)
Stewards	: Miss Jones' team of year 5 & 6 helpers
Display	: Mr Morris and year 3
Lighting	: Miss West and Mr Sheach

● *A checklist*

Keep this handy such as on the bulletin board in the school entrance. It keeps people up to date and shows your powers of organisation.

The keyword is DELEGATION
Here's an example of a checklist

ITEM	NAME	ACTION	DATE FOR COMPLETION	COMPLETION
Lighting	Miss West	Check existing lights.	12/10/96	✔
		Rig & colour	12/11/96	✔
		Hire/borrow	09/09/96	✔
	Mr Sheach	Get help from Art Centre technician	12/11/96	
Press release	Class 6	Write it.	18/11/96	
	Mrs Burgess	Check it	25/11/96	
		send to Gazette	05/12/96	
	Mr Caveen	Display in foyer		
Refreshments	PTA – Mrs Payne	Organise helpers	05/12/96	✔
		Equipment?		✔
		Urn?		✔
		Cakes		✔
		3 lots of help		✔

BUDGETING

Some handy hints
- plan it
- decide on needs
- discuss it with head/staff/PTA
- delegate
- other routes..........

Planning

- Decide on a budget request. Try to base it on realistic figures with some contingency measures.

Needs

- Do an audit of the performances needs e.g. how many lights need hiring?
    Make-up requirements?
    Photocopying of programmes?
    Refreshment costs?
    Video hire or charges?
- Think ahead.

Discussion

- Find out what is available.
- Find out what you may need to borrow from PTA/school fund.
- Can you raise funds e.g. a raffle or sponsored silence.
- Find out the situation.

Delegate

- Ask your school administration team for their advice and financial expertise. They will know the mystery of the financial procedures in vogue, the horrors of VAT, the pitfalls of local purchase.
- Ask for one member of this invaluable team to handle the performance budget.
- Find out about invoices which may be raised for equipment such as lighting.
- Can you nip out and buy a metre of ribbon and then claim the cash? Check procedures.
- If you intend to sell tickets, checkout legal requirements.
- Request a regular financial breakdown.
- If you make a profit, request a performance fund is set up for the next event!

Other routes

- Local shops and suppliers may donate equipment in return for a credit in the programme.
- Delegate the task of exploring local community help in donating equipment to a colleague.
- The Local Art Centre may loan equipment and expertise.
- Large firms such as banks and building societies may give help in the form of finance or equipment. Check if there are any parental links.
- Local press or radio stations could give out requests for equipment and help to promote the event!
- If it is a big event, checkout local authority grants for performance projects.
- TShirts and performance memorabilia e.g. caps/keyrings/pens....
  Do calculate accurately and cost approximately so you breakeven or make a profit.
- Searching for help with equipment could be a useful vehicle for local study work in geography. See if it fits into a class topic and then delegate!

PROJECT TIMETABLE

Before you have your first meeting, try to plan the timetable for the performance event. It will give you a clearer idea of time scale and you can also see where dates may clash with other events.

Don't forget to put in vital dates such as half term/end of term/day closures etc.

The keyword is: PLANNING

Here's an example.

PROJECT TIMETABLE for SERPENT KING with Junior Drama Club

DATE	AIM	ACTION POINTS
Week 1	To get pupils interested	Call lunchtime meeting for pupils. Explain project and jobs. Book - hall. Set dates for after school rehearsal.
Week 2	• 5 headed monster • Staff briefing	1st rehearsal - create 5 headed monster. Tell staff and ask for help. Money!
Week 3	Communication • Story line started	• Bulletin board • Parents evening - ask for help • Meeting of helpers - contact outside help • Story mapped in still images
Week 4	Keep momentum	• Cast parts. VIPs letters out. • Start masks - delegate • Book lighting - delegate
Week 5	HALF TERM	
Week 6	Rehearsal 1 x lunch 1 x pm	• Masks. Invite locals to watch • Dance input from local Asian theatre group • Costumes - delegate
Week 7	Rehearsals - getting a flow	• Narrator script • Masks and moves • Production meeting - PTA refreshments
Week 8	Rehearsals Organisation	• Check organisation for event • Use masks with moves • Music? Video? - delegate
Week 9	Dress rehearsals	• Pupils from classes, 2 afternoons • Costume check • Press contact • Masks. Can we see and hear them? • Lighting arrives.
Week 10	PERFORMANCE	2 nights 5th/6th December 1 afternoon 4th December Return lights.
Week 11	Thank you's	• Return lights • Watch video • Thank you's • Relax!

DATE/WEEK	AIM	ACTION POINTS

A blank form for your use

CHECKLIST

THIS MAY HELP TOWARDS THE SMOOTH ORGANISATION OF YOUR SCHOOL PERFORMANCE

ACOUSTICS — Check your performance space. Can you hear your performers? If you have a stage do not use it just because it's there! Find ingenious staging approaches so every line is heard clearly.

AUDIENCE — Make sure everyone can see the performers in action. Do invite your Governors; Local Education Officers; Inspectors; Teacher Advisers, as well as parents. Extend your invitation to the local community and Senior Citizens groups. It builds on good school/community relations and helps P.R.

BACKSTAGE — Engage staff and helpers to aid backstage. Make sure they know the running order of events. Keep performers out of sight until the start if you can. Make sure performers are occupied whilst they await their turn e.g. quiet games/books.

BLOCKS — Rosta blocks can make a good low stage or extend an existing stage. They must be kept in good repair. They should not be sited in front of low windows. Batten blocks together so they do not drift apart in mid-scene. Check the noise level when performers walk on them. See if you can borrow from a neighbouring school or Arts Centre.

BUDGET — Negotiate a budget with your Head for items. Keep clear accounts. Ask your finance officer to help. They know the system!

CARETAKER — Cherish your caretaker. They can make or break a show! Keep them informed. Ask for their expertise. Include them on the list of VIPs and give them a credit in the programme.

CLEANERS — Keep them informed so they do not appear mid-show to clean the floor!

COLLECTION POINT — Allocate one area of the school to collect performers. This avoids confusion; parents getting in the way; lost performers; parents appearing mid-show to collect their charges. A classroom or library is adequate.

COMMUNITY — Invite community groups to your show. Good PR. If your school is used for adult education classes, do liaise with the organiser to avoid confusion; wrangles over the piano or the Yoga Class taking over the hall during the evening of your show. If they use other rooms do have plenty of signs indicating their rooms.

COSTUMES — Your local Theatrical Wardrobe are willing to oblige but do give PLENTY of notice. In school, give each performer a hanger and an indestructible label. All costumes go on hanger and are stored at a central collection point. A hanging rail is handy. Delegate a costume storage job. Keep a list of costumes. Have plenty of safety pins ready.

CRECHE — This can be a useful arrangement to allow parents with toddlers a bit of peace in which to watch their elder charges. Keeps the audience happy too. Proper qualified supervision is vital.

DELEGATE — Allocate jobs to pupils and colleagues. Do not try to do it all yourself. Hold regular meetings to check on progress. Pupils, not in the play, can thrive on this responsibility. Everyone, then has a part to play.

DISPLAY — School shows are a perfect opportunity to show off class and individual work. Early arrivers (and the collection point) can be deposited in a classroom or library to look at the display. (Make sure it's up to date)

FIRE — Vital that staff, helpers, performers and stewards know the fire drill. Fire extinguishers to be clearly sited. Exit signs must be visible and well lit. Do not block exits with audience seats. Parents sometimes move chairs for a better view! Be firm.

FOYER — Use this area for displays of work and photographs relating to the show. Your PTA could sell school goodies and/or refreshments if there is space. Use this space carefully. It is a focal point. Have stewards at the main doors to guide the audience.

HEALTH & SAFETY
- Every teacher has a duty to ensure that the working
- environment complies with Health and Safety regulations laid down by the County and that pupils are supervised in the use of equipment. When in doubt, consult the Health and Safety Rep. in your school.

HEATING — **Make sure:**
In the winter, for evening shows, that it is on.
In the summer it is off!
Does the noise of the system drown the performers?.
Check details with your Caretaker (an expert in these matters).
Has the school budgeted for extra heating during evening events?

JOBS — Keep a "Jobs for the Day" bulletin board so everyone involved is kept informed. Put it in a visible location so parents and visitors can see the information.

LIGHTING — If you are going to use stage lighting, you must follow these regulations...
(1) It must be regularly inspected and maintained.
(2) It must be fitted with safety chains.
(3) It must be hung from properly fitted lighting bars or approved lighting stands.
(4) Do not overload your lighting grid.
(5) If you are hanging lanterns, use a scaffolding tower or a stepladder with rubber feet (held by a second person).
(6) Switch off power supply when hanging lanterns.
(7) Wear leather gloves when hanging lanterns.
(8) Colour filters must be cinemoid.
(9) No dangling cables.

— If you are hiring or borrowing equipment do check that the equipment is wired by a professional electrician. If in doubt, contact your local authority electrical unit for help. Fire extinguishers must be placed by the lighting box.

LOO — Put up clear signs for pupils, staff and audience. Make sure performers go beforehand

MONEY — If you charge for tickets, the school takes on a legal responsibility for the safety of the public. Delegate the money job to a trustee. Check in which school account money can be kept. (Do not keep money yourself) Keep clear accounts.

NEXT DAY — Check if the performance space needs clearing for assembly/PE/lunch. Organise a removal team.

PARKING	– Put up clear signs to avoid confusion. State space available in a letter to parents. Do not block exits. Is the parking area lit at night? Consult your Caretaker. Check time for locking gates too. Use pupils to direct parking and escort visitors to the correct entrance.
PERFORMERS	– Keep them calm. Brief them clearly about performance day arrangements, timings, changing rooms, loos, refreshments, etc. Have a regular roll call. Have understudy arrangements ready. Keep your temper and smile a lot.
PHOTOGRAPHS	– Take plenty and use them in the foyer display. Sell copies. All proceeds to your school account. Arrange for staff, parent or local secondary school to take them for you. Budget for them. If possible, allocate **one** performance for parents to take photos of their charges. It is off-putting to have constant flashes and whirrings mid-show. Encourage parents to leave cameras at home and buy from your display.
PROGRAMME	– Get pupils to design and make the programme. Ensure the names of all performers and helpers are included, spelt correctly. Credit all who have helped; donated equipment; the Caretaker etc. Advertise the next school events.
PROPS	– Delegate the job to a trusted pupil. All props to be kept in clearly labelled boxes after the show. During the show, an accessible props table (labelled) is vital.
PUBLICITY	– Have lots. A good money spinner if you make badges or T-shirts. Get pupils to design these plus posters and hand bills. Distribute to local shops and Art Centres. Prepare a press-release and organise local papers to record the event.
RECORD OF THE EVENT	– Keep all photos; press cuttings in a glossy folder for display at open days; inspections and parents events.
REFRESHMENTS	– Delegate to the PTA, pupils or local secondary school (a good technology project). Everyone loves a cuppa (or something stronger). Another moneyspinner. Make sure the hot water urn is switched on in good time too!
SCENERY	– All drapes and scenery must be treated with an appropriate fire-retardant substance. Ensure scenery is looked after by your stage management team. This could be a project for your local secondary school!
SEATING	– All seats must be linked together for safety. Ensure the performers can be seen from your seating arrangements. Infant chairs don't suit all bottoms!
SECONDARY LINKS	– Use your show to reinforce links with your feeder schools. They can use the show for their own projects in technology and the Arts or Technology and business studies. They can also loan you equipment.
SIGNS	– Have plenty to show the Way in/Way out/loos/refreshments/No entry/Fire exits/'phone/parking.
STEWARDS	– Use pupils to show audience to their seats; to greet VIPs. Make sure they are fully briefed on fire regulations. Give them badges to signify their important job.
TAPES	– If you use sound equipment check it all works. Check volume required. (Do not seat anyone near speakers!) If using music or effects, carefully label each tape. If possible have one tape per piece required. Store carefully too. Make copies in case of loss.

TECHNICAL	– Ensure any technical equipment is used with full knowledge of Health and Safety regulations. Your local authority officer can help.
THANK YOU'S	– Send a note/card/gift as appropriate to all helpers. It helps maintain goodwill for the next time.
TIMINGS	– Be sensible. Allocate time for the show, bearing in mind the age of performers and state of the audience. Have an interval if appropriate. Concentration spans vary. A good show is not necessarily a long show. State timings in the programme. Remember that you, your pupils and colleagues may have to be at school the next day.
TRANSPORT	– Make sure all performers and helpers have transport home if it is an evening show. Delegate one member of staff to round up and deliver strays. If it is a day show, do finish by the time school ends or else make clear arrangements.
VIPs	– Invite by letter. Request RSVP. Allocate a steward to babysit them.
VIDEO	– Record the show. This could be a good media education project for your pupils or for your local secondary school. Sell the video! Again, allocate one performance for parents to video their charges. The constant whirring and clicking; the gymnastic exploits of would-be Spielbergs recording their offspring can be very distracting, so find a way of preventing this (like banning them).
WINE OR ANY OTHER APPROPRIATE BEVERAGE.	– A welcome refreshment after the event. Do have plenty to share. A bottle opener helps. Invite all your willing helpers if appropriate. Make sure you have a lift home!

Please add to this list as you learn from experience!

Good luck.

SURVIVAL TIPS

PLANNING	Plan well in advance
PREPARATION	Be clear about the performance you want.
DELEGATION	Get help : build on pupils and colleagues expertise. You cannot do everything!
COMMUNICATION	Keep everyone informed via short, precise meetings and a school bulletin board.
ORGANISATION	A little organisation goes a long way.

Remember: a good performance lasts a lifetime in the memory of your school and your pupils.

KEEP CALM
KEEP IT SIMPLE
ENJOY THE EVENT
KEEP SMILING

INDEX

(Italic type indicates where a definition can be found)

Access, on and off stage 37, 41
Acoustics 99
Activating strategies 9, 10
Arts Council 4-6
Art, as curriculum subject 17, 31, 48, 64, 83
Artefacts
 The Great Exhibition 51
Assembly, school 8, 101
Audience 25, 41, 58, 99
 attention 56
 participation 46, 78
 response 6
Avenue (staging position) 27

Backstage 99
Barndoors 37, *38*, 40
Balinese puppet 81
Batten 38
Blocks, for stage 99
Budgeting 96, 99

Caretaker 99-101
Carols, use of 21
Celebrations 6, 15, 20, 51, 78
Characters
 Dear Greenpeace 33
 Great Exhibition 51, 53
 Serpent King 69
Checklist
 of organisation 99-100
 of performance procedure 95
 stage lighting 37
Children with learning difficulties 81
Chorus 9, 11, 22, 70, 77, 92
Cinderella 9-11
Cleaners 99
Collection point, of performers 99
Communication 94
 non-verbal 62
Community, effect of performance on 99
Cost
 lighting 40
Costume 23-24, 99
 Dear Greenpeace 42
 Great Exhibition 57
 Nativity 25
 Serpent King 77
Craftpacks 79
Creche 99
Cross-curricular links 6, 7, 14, 16, 31, 48, 64, 83
Crystal Palace 46, 47, 54

Dance 15, 17, 31, 48, 62, 64, 78
 as curriculum subject 83
Delegation, of jobs 95, 96, 99, 100
Dialogue 9, 11, 35, 62, 78
Director 20, 94
Display 100
Divali 15
Drama, as curriculum subject 17, 31, 48
Dramatic Curriculum 18, 32, 49, 65, 84
Drama screen 27, 85
Dress rehearsal 24, 28

English, curriculum subject 31, 64, 83
Equipment
 drama screen 27, 85
End on 26
Environment, subject for drama 32
 see also 'Dear Greenpeace'
Entrance 25
Exit 25

Fact File, The Great Exhibition 50
Factsheet, character 53
Festivals 15
Fights, in drama 78
Finance, of performances 96, 100
Fire, precaution 100
Five year olds 70
Folktale
 Asian 62
Foyer 24, 100
Flashback 21
Floodlight 38
Fresnel 38
Front of House 94, 100
Frozen picture technique 8, 12, 22

Geography, curriculum subject 17, 31, 48, 64, 83
Gesture 4, 9, 11, 35, 62
Great Exhibition, The 7, 45-60
Greek theatre, staging position 26
Greenpeace 6, 29-44
Gobbo 36, *39*, 40

Health and safety 30, 100, 102
Heating 100
Help points 12, 24, 28, 34
Hindu religion 15
History, as curriculum subject 7, 17, 48, 64, 83
Hotseating 53

Images 71
Improvisation 4, 6, 14, 18, 35
In the round, staging position 26
Instant Assembly model 7, 8-12, 18
 secret formula 10

Jobs, for a performance 100

Kaliya 66-69
Krishna 66-69
Key stage 1: 4, 16, 18, 32, 49
Key stage 2: 4, 7, 16, 18, 30, 32, 49, 65

Language, curriculum subject 17, 48
Lanterns 38, 39
Loos 100
Lighting 37-40, 41, 85, 95, 97, 100
 cost 40
 resources 44, 95

Mahabarata 81, 84
Making (expressing ideas) 6
Make-up 75
Making a puppet 87

103

Maths, curriculum subject 17, 48
Masks 22, 25, 62
  making 73-75
  project 7
  types 75
Mime 4, 9, 11, 22, 23, 35, 62, 67, 70, 77
Mothering Sunday 15
Movement 4, 9, 62, 75, 77
Music
  as curriculum subject 16, 17, 31, 46, 48, 64, 83
  in performance 42, 55, 58, 70, 78, 86
  instruments 15, 81

Narrator 10, 20, 21
  The Great Exhibition 46, 55, 59
  Serpent King 62, 67, 77
  The Shadow Puppet 86, 92
National Curriculum 4, 7, 16, 18, 32, 40, 49, 51, 65, 84 see also key stages
Nativity 6, 16-28
Non-verbal communication 62 see also gesture, mime and movement
Nursery rhymes 84

Organisation 93
Overhead projection
  Nativity 22
  Greenpeace 36
  Great Exhibition 54, 55, 59
  Shadow Puppets 85-86

PE, curriculum subject 48
  mats 7
Papier mâché 74
Pantomime 72
Parcan lantern 39, 85
Parents
  as audience 25
  involvement 5, 51, 94, 96-102
Parking 100
Performance 5, 14,
  Hints 86
Performing platform
  Dear Greenpeace 34
Personal and social education 31
Photographs 101
Physical imaging 12, 54
Preparation 103
Pre-recorded sound 42
Pre-school group 23
Press release 95, 96, 101
Prince Albert 50, 55, 56
Production techniques
  Nativity 25
  Great Exhibition 57
  The Serpent King 72
  Shadow Puppet 85
Promenade, staging position 27
Projector see Overhead projection
Profile spot 39
Programmes 95, 101
Props 101
  Dear Greenpeace 36
  Great Exhibition 58
Publicity 101
Puppeteers 86
Puppets 81-91

Queen Victoria 51, 55, 56

RE, curriculum subject 17, 48, 64, 83
Ramayana 81, 84

Record of the event 101
Refreshments 101, 102
Rehearsal 8, 10, 14, 20, 28, 67, 94
  dress 24, 28
  of songs 19

Religions
  Christian 14
  festivals 15
  Hindu 62
Research 15, 18, 46, 51
Resources
  Great Exhibition 60
  lights 40
  sound effects 44
Roles 57
  accessories for 57
  non-speaking, see Still images
Roles and responsibilities 94
Running order
  Nativity 21
  Dear Greenpeace 35
  The Great Exhibition 55

SCAA 4
Safety 37, 40, 41, 46, 86, 100-102
Science, curriculum subject 17, 31, 48, 83
Screen, see drama screen
Script 14, 18, 20, 50, 53, 78, 84
Seating 10, 25-27, 58, 99
Secondary links 101
Shadow puppets
  creating shadows 85
  history 81
  making 87-91
  staging 92
Signs 94, 100, 101
Skills 5, 9, 18, 28, 46
Spoken thoughts 9, 11, 23, 46, 55, 70
Slow motion 9, 11, 70, 77, 78
Song 19, 21, 46, 58, 59, 67
Sound effects 41, 44
Sound
  live 41
  pre-recorded 42
Staging 25
  positions 26
Stage manager 94
Stewards 101
Still images 9, 10, 14, 62, 70
Strategies 70

Tableau 19, 20, 24
Tapes 42, 102
Technology 7, 17, 31, 48, 64, 83
Tension, dramatic 56

Thrust, stage position 26
Thank you's 102
Timetable 97-98
Timings 102
Topic work 7, 14, 15, 19
Transport 102
Tu B'Shevat 15

Upstage 78

Video 10, 28, 35, 102
VIPs 101, 102

Wings 85

Yuantan 15